# DATE DUE

| OC 1 7 00 | | | |
|---|---|---|---|
| JE 2 0 '72 | | | |
| | | | |
| | | | |
| | | | |
| | | | |
| | | | |
| | | | |
| | | | |
| | | | |
| | | | |
| | | | |
| | | | |
| | | | |
| | | | |
| | | | |
| | | | |
| | | | |

D0572758

# Perceptions of Animals

# in American Culture

Edited by R. J. Hoage

Smithsonian Institution Press   Washington, D.C.   London

© 1989 Smithsonian Institution
All rights reserved

Library of Congress Cataloging-in-
Publication Data

Perceptions of animals in American
culture.
Bibliography: p.
1. Animals and civilization—United
States.
2. Animals—Social aspects—United
States.
I. Hoage, R. J.
QL85.P44 1989    591'.0973    89-600054
ISBN 0-87474-493-8 (alk. paper)

British Library Cataloging-in-Publication
Data available
Manufactured in the United States of
America

10  9  8  7  6  5  4  3  2  1

∞ The paper used in this publication
meets the minimum requirements of the
American National Standard for
Permanence of Paper for Printed Library
Materials Z39.48-1984.

*Edited by Marian K. Coombs*
*Designed by Lisa Buck Vann*

## National Zoological Park Symposia for the Public

This series brings before the public a variety of intriguing and controversial issues in wildlife biology and conservation. Complicated topics are addressed. Problems are analyzed. In many cases, solutions are offered and discussed. The goal of these books is to provide information to stimulate public awareness and debate of the problems that animals and their habitats face in a world increasingly dominated by human beings.

To Patti,

who sees music as the solution,

who knows the meaning of the word "fun,"

and who makes a house

worth coming home to;

and to Larry,

who helps keep the perceptions

where they should be.

# Contents

# Contents

# Contributors

Steve Barnett
Research and Forecasts, Inc.
110 East 59th Street
New York, New York 10023

Joel Berger
Department of Range, Wildlife and
  Forestry
College of Agriculture
University of Nevada-Reno
Reno, Nevada 89512

Gordon Burghardt
Department of Psychology
University of Tennessee
Knoxville, Tennessee 37996

David Challinor
Science Advisor to the Secretary and
Former Assistant Secretary for
  Science
Smithsonian Institution
Washington, D.C. 20560

Harold Herzog, Jr.
Department of Psychology
Western Carolina University
Cullowhee, North Carolina 28723

Robert J. Hoage
National Zoological Park
Smithsonian Institution
Washington, D.C. 20008

Aaron Katcher
School of Dentistry
4001 Spruce Street
University of Pennsylvania
Philadelphia, Pennsylvania 19104

Stephen Kellert
School of Forestry and Environmental
    Studies
Sage Hall
Yale University
205 Prospect Street
New Haven, Connecticut 06511

Erich Klinghammer
Department of Psychology
Purdue University
West Lafayette, Indiana 47907

Elizabeth Lawrence
Department of Environmental Studies
School of Veterinary Medicine
Tufts University
Medford, Massachusetts 02155

Randall Lockwood
The Humane Society of the United
    States
2100 L Street, N.W.
Washington, D.C. 20037

JoAnn Magdoff
41 Central Park West
New York, New York 10023

Lilly-Marlene Russow
Department of Philosophy
Purdue University
West Lafayette, Indiana 47907

# Preface

**R. J. Hoage**

Perhaps the greatest challenge confronting a wildlife educator is to encourage people to see animals "as animals"—that is, without prejudice or preconceived notions or anthropomorphic projections. This goal would seem to be all but impossible to achieve given the bombardment of humanized animal characters to which we all are subjected. Perhaps most notable are the anthropomorphized creatures that abound on the comic pages of our newspapers, reaching hundreds of millions of people daily. On television a koala tells us to fly a certain airline, penguins try to persuade us to drink a particular kind of diet cola, and dogs complain they are being lied to when given anything but one specific brand of dog food. From boxes on supermarket shelves, tigers, toucans, and rabbits all tout their brand of cereal. On posters, a bloodhound cautions us to watch out for criminals in our neighborhoods. And of course Smokey the Bear exhorts us, "Only *you* can prevent forest fires!"

There are many more examples like these in twentieth-century American society. Faced with such a barrage, how can educators reach adults and children with messages that convey the ways animals truly live and behave?

Environmentalist/songwriter Bill "Billy B" Brennan of Washington, D.C., has taken up the challenge. In a song that has become well known around Washington, he describes a boy and a girl who visit a pond to feed the ducks. While throwing out bread, the children hear the cries of a duck that is running for its life from a fox. The alarmed boy exclaims, "Ooh, he's mean!" The fox stops in his tracks and explains, "I'm not mean, I'm just hungry! Hungry as I can be! That duck looks cute to you, but he looks like food to me!" Billy B's song, "I'm Not Mean, I'm Just Hungry,"* of course, projects human thought processes and speech onto the fox, but the lyrics help people realize that a fox kills and eats its prey without malice, in order to survive. If foxes, lions, tigers, and other carnivores are to exist in nature they must kill and eat other animals, and we should not vilify their predatory natures.

The fact that the duck in the song is considered "cute" makes it difficult for the boy to understand that the duck could also be viewed as food. How humans have come to see some animals as "cute" or "adorable" and others as "mean" or "treacherous" is a topic that has long perplexed biologists.

One animal that has been maligned since the beginning of western civilization is the snake. There are many negative references to snakes in the Bible, chief among them the serpent's temptation of Eve in the Garden of Eden, which resulted in snakes being "cursed above all cattle and every beast of the field" (Gen. 3:14). The image stuck. In a survey of visitors conducted at the National Zoo, the majority of respondents stated they did not dislike any animal in particular, but a highly opinionated

---

*© 1984; used with author's permission.

minority (27 percent) asserted that they disliked snakes and other reptiles. No other animal or group of animals was disliked by so many people. The perception that snakes are evil and treacherous has been perpetuated in our culture even though there is some evidence that the loathing of snakes is not necessarily innate in humans; many children as young as three-and-a-half years of age show no "instinctive" fear of snakes (Pinney 1981).* So, on the one hand, the loathing of snakes appears to be a learned response, an artifact of our culture, but on the other, Burghardt and Herzog (this volume) argue that a genetically prescribed fear of snakes would have been of adaptive value given the sizeable number of venomous species. At this time the jury awaits further testimony.

In contrast to snakes and other reptiles, the preferred animal of those who expressed a favorite in the National Zoo visitor survey was the giant panda (25 percent). Giant pandas are often described as "cute, cuddly, and adorable." Why creatures that have certain physical characteristics similar to giant pandas—relatively flat faces, short limbs, eyes that appear large—are labeled "cute" is a topic pursued in this volume.

The perceptions of animals in American culture have been influenced by innumerable factors, including myths, folklore, the frontier experience, religion, changes in economics and social structure, inventions, politics, philosophy, wildlife research, zoos, the press, films and television, and the conservation and animal rights movements. In discussions with scientists working at the National Zoological Park, I found that many, including myself, felt that a symposium on perceptions of animals in our society would generate a very useful examination of how these perceptions have arisen and how they have evolved as a result of changing historical contexts. It was difficult to decide where to start and how much material could be included; there is an immense amount of exciting information on the topic. The chapters in this volume, taken from symposium presentations, attempt to cover the major influences on Americans' perceptions of animals.

---

*Pinney, R. 1981. *The snake book*. Garden City, N.Y.: Doubleday.

# Overview

David Challinor introduces the book's nine chapters by examining the human propensity to project positive and negative human attributes onto animate and inanimate objects. He also discusses how zoos are trying to minimize anthropomorphic perceptions by exhibiting animals in near-natural settings. Stephen Kellert explores how perceptual categories are defined and how public attitudes toward animals must be taken into account when wildlife education and conservation programs are created. Lilly-Marlene Russow reviews how perceptions of animals in America have changed over the last one hundred fifty years. She emphasizes the influence of urbanization and other historical and intellectual developments that have resulted in the modern, romanticized view of animals. Randall Lockwood examines the question, Can anthropomorphic projections be a service to animals by helping educators instill in members of the public a better understanding of animal behavior and biology, or are such projections an archaic tendency of no further value? Elizabeth Lawrence looks at attitudes toward animals in several different cultures, especially the extent to which certain cultures anthropomorphize animals. She also explores how "neoteny"—the retention in adults of infantile and juvenile characteristics—has a significant influence on American perceptions of animals. Erich Klinghammer discusses one of the most misrepresented and misunderstood animals on this planet—the wolf. He examines the misinformation about wolves that has been perpetuated for years, and he considers how subtle changes are now taking place in public attitudes toward the wolf. JoAnn Magdoff and Steve Barnett examine advertising strategies involving animals and how people perceive animals in the context of current American cultural trends. Joel Berger explores the positive image that horses traditionally have had in American culture—in contradistinction to the wolf—an image, however, that in certain circumstances can clearly be reversed. Aaron Katcher explains that some human psychological needs may be met by how animals make us feel and that these feelings play an important role in human–animal interactions. Finally, this book concludes with an analysis by Gordon Burghardt and Harold Herzog, who discuss the drawbacks of using anthropomorphic approaches in the development of ethical guidelines for human relationships with other species. They also look at the possible evolutionary origins for some of the behaviors humans exhibit toward animals.

I think you, the reader, will find this volume intriguing and thought-provoking. I hope it will stimulate some self-analysis that may make you aware of the biases we all have toward animals, and perhaps make you consider how these biases can affect the decisions that determine public policy toward wildlife.

# Acknowledgments

Funds from the Friends of the National Zoo (FONZ) and another organization that prefers to remain anonymous made possible the National Zoological Park's "Perceptions of Animals in American Culture" symposium and the publication of this book. I am very grateful for their support.

Thanks must go to the National Zoo's Office of Public Affairs staff—Michael Morgan, Margie Gibson, Ilene Ackerman, Tabetha Carpenter, and, especially, Sally French—for their dedication to the production of the symposium and this volume. I also would like to thank National Zoo assistant director Chris Wemmer for his support of the symposium in its early stages, director Mike Robinson for supporting the concept of the public symposia series and publication of their proceedings, and Theresa Slowik and Diane Bohmhauer for their editorial and production support.

Finally, I am pleased that artists Sally Bensusen, Richard Swartz, and Vichai Malikul could provide so many of the outstanding illustrations that complement the information presented here.

# Introduction: Contrasting Viewpoints

**David Challinor**

Animals have always played a very important role in the lives and thoughts of humans. Throughout history people have tried to understand animals and incorporate them into their changing conceptions of the world. Depending on what period and which culture one is looking at, one can find animals being viewed as gods, demons, machines, tools, children, prophets, and in many other ways. However, the theme that appears repeatedly in the human characterization of animals is anthropomorphism—the projection onto animals of our own feelings, thoughts, motives, and other human qualities. It is a theme that will be mentioned by several of the authors in this book.

The urge to humanize—to explain things in terms of human experience—is so strong that even inanimate objects are perceived in terms of human attributes: Hurricanes, ships, trains, machinery, houses, and mountains have all been given names and personalities at one time or another. Our ancestors even organized the cosmos in human terms. Looking out at the unfathomable universe, the ancients perceived humanlike gods as the cause of all things and events. Natural objects and animals took on human personalities. The projection of human traits onto nature seems to have made the world more understandable and the unknown more familiar. Even today, with our scientific understanding of the world, Americans continue to anthropomorphize, especially in our perceptions of animals. Surely this behavior must be fulfilling an important need within us.

But our perceptions and attitudes, however they may have evolved, affect our interaction with nature and thus our impact on the natural world. And as the natural world shrinks, we need to better understand our attitudes and how they shape our actions. Although today, in America, the most common way of perceiving animals is based on anthropomorphic projections, there exist other perceptions as well, as Stephen Kellert will explain later in this volume. Differing perspectives on animals are most clearly seen in the controversies surrounding such programs as seal hunting, coyote baiting, and animal biomedical research. Such controversies arise precisely because each side defines and colors issues differently. Dilemmas like these may never get resolved until we learn more about why contradictory viewpoints exist and how they have arisen. That is one of the reasons for this volume.

Differing attitudes toward animals cause dilemmas for zoos, too, but in less controversial ways. On the one hand, modern zoos, with their emphasis on research, education, and conservation, are increasingly attempting to promote what Kellert (this volume) calls the ecologistic perspective. One way they do this is by exhibiting animals in as natural a setting as possible and in numbers approximating natural group sizes in the wild. In some zoos a number of different species that ordinarily live in the same climatic zone are exhibited together in order to simulate one large ecological system, such as the African plains. Of course, a simulation is not the same as the wild, but it gives viewers the sense of how an ecosystem works.

# Introduction

At the same time, some zoos have had a tradition of being more like stationary circuses in which animals are given names, have tea parties, and provide rides to children. Once animals are removed from naturalistic settings and social groups, it is easy for human spectators to forget their wild nature and to anthropomorphize them. But which type of environment best serves the animals: the one that anthropomorphizes them or the one that emphasizes their natural behaviors and adaptations? The zoo community is clearly still grappling with this dilemma. An interesting example of the contrasting elements of this debate can be found in a promotional videotape issued by the American Association of Zoological Parks and Aquariums in 1983 to increase public interest in zoos. This tape undoubtedly attracted additional people to zoos, but it also reflects the ambiguity of the zoo association's position on how zoos should be presented to the public. In the tape, all the animals were presented in naturalistic environments. The enclosures were large and spacious, and the animals were separated from people by moats or glass panels—not old-fashioned prisonlike bars. The group sizes were very natural and seemed to reflect what might be seen in the wild. All these characteristics are among the best features of modern zoos. But at the same time, through the use of clever editing and dubbing, the animals appeared to be talking, joking, singing, and generally acting like human characters. So this is the dilemma we face: To what extent is the new emphasis on naturalism or ecology at odds with older, anthropomorphic traditions? Are these apparently contrasting approaches to stimulating public interest mutually exclusive, or can they be blended in some way in order to attract people and then educate them about how the animals live in their natural environments? There is no definitive answer yet, but it is a pivotal question.

The positive and negative aspects of anthropomorphic projections as well as other dilemmas found in human–animal interrelationships are subjects for discussion in this volume. Anyone interested in gaining an understanding of the origins of these dilemmas will benefit considerably by reading the chapters that follow.

# Perceptions of Animals
# in America

**Stephen R. Kellert**

Among the most basic problems in analyzing perceptions of animals is the creation of a discrete set of categories that permit both the description of and measurement of fundamental human attitudes toward animals. Beginning in 1973 and continuing over several years, a typology of basic attitudes was developed, followed by studies to determine the presence and strength of such attitude categories among a diverse group of Americans in the forty-eight contiguous states and Alaska (Kellert 1974, 1976, 1978, 1979, 1980a, 1980b).

The attitude categories primarily describe basic perceptions rather than behaviors. Attitudes should *not* be identified with individual people— that is, attitudes may describe elements of a person's perception, but rarely will all of an individual's actions be explained by just one attitude. Moreover, the attitudes held by an individual may change over time as the person experiences different life situations. Nevertheless, in nearly every individual, a certain degree of attitude stability is encountered, and in most people the attitudes are hierarchically ordered according to primary, secondary, and tertiary importance. Below, ten attitudes toward animals are defined in some detail.

# Attitude Categories

### The Naturalistic Attitude

The primary characteristic of this attitude is a strong interest in and affection for the outdoors and wildlife. Active contact with natural settings is especially valued; thus the naturalistic attitude is closely related to both the wilderness and the outdoor recreational benefits of wildlife. A sense of permanence, simplicity, and pleasure derived from unspoiled natural beauty is typically associated with this perspective. Most of all, observation and personal involvement with wildlife are key to the naturalistic interest in the outdoors, with animals providing the context and meaning for active participation in natural settings. Thus wildlife offers the intellectual content and challenge for seeking the outdoors and wilderness experience.

### The Ecologistic Attitude

Like the naturalistic, the ecologistic attitude focuses primarily on wildlife. The essential differences, however, are the degree of personal involvement, recreational interest, and the importance attached to an intellectual understanding of nature. The ecologistic emphasis is directed at a systematic conceptual understanding of the interrelationships of species in the context of ecosystems, with major concern for dependencies between animals and their natural habitats, in contrast to the naturalistic concern for personal, often recreational, involvement with specific animals. Additionally, the ecologistic approach shifts the focus of attention from individual animals to the behaviors of large numbers of wildlife species. Wild animals are valued not so much as sources of affection or amusement, but as devices for comprehending the broader functionings of natural systems—in other words, as barometers of natural-system health or disturbance.

## The Humanistic Attitude

This attitude primarily emphasizes feelings of strong affection and attachment to individual animals, typically pets. The animal is the recipient of feelings and emotional projections somewhat analogous to those expressed toward other people. No amount of affection for animals, however, can compensate for intrinsic biological differences, and thus the animal is rendered something of a subhuman. Nevertheless, the humanistic attitude values animals primarily as basic sources of affection and companionship and, for some persons, even as surrogate humans. Considerable empathy for animal emotion and thought typically accompanies this perspective; consequently, anthropomorphic distortions can result. The attributes and capacities of animals may be idealized, leading to somewhat romanticized notions of animal innocence and virtue. The humanistic attitude toward wildlife usually involves strong affection for animals phylogenetically close to human beings, as well as for those animals that are large and aesthetically attractive. Since the humanistic concern is for individual animals, species considerations relating to population dynamics typically are disregarded.

## The Moralistic Attitude

The primary concern of the moralistic attitude is for the ethically appropriate human treatment of animals. Like the ecologistic attitude, it involves as much a state of mind as any personal, behavioral, or recreational involvement with actual animals. While the moralistic attitude is often associated with feelings of strong affection for animals, its more fundamental characteristic is a philosophical emphasis on the nature of appropriate human conduct toward the nonhuman world. Perhaps the most basic tenet of the moralistic attitude is strong opposition to inflicting pain, harm, or suffering on animals. Exploitation of animals in the interest of human amusement or gain, without extreme justification or necessity, is regarded as ethically wrong and cruel. A basic moralistic principle is the fundamental equality of all animals, each endowed with an inalienable right to existence. The moralistic focus dictates a commitment to protect other forms of sentient life from human domination and exploitation, except in situations where human survival is at stake or to serve "higher" ends (e.g., to protect other creatures).

## The Scientistic Attitude

The predominant concerns of the scientistic attitude are the biological and physical characteristics of animals. This perspective values animals largely as objects of curiosity, study, and observation. While not necessarily resulting in a lack of affection for animals, the scientistic attitude often fosters feelings of emotional detachment; wildlife are primarily of interest as generators of questions that demand answers, not as sources of companionship or wilderness recreation. A reductionist outlook may result, viewing animal life more in terms of basic processes—constituent parts—than as living creatures in relationship to other animals in the context of natural environments.

## The Aesthetic Attitude

This attitude primarily emphasizes the attractiveness or symbolic significance of animals. The major concern is with the artistic merit and beauty of animals, or their allegorical appeal as bearers of some special message.

## The Utilitarian Attitude

The fundamental attribute of the utilitarian attitude is a concern with the practical and material value of animals—imputing significance to animals based primarily on their usefulness to people. A basic presumption is that animals should serve some human purpose and therefore contribute to personal gain. This attitude does not necessarily result in an indifference to or lack of affection for animals, but emotional considerations are usually subordinated to more practical demands for human material benefit.

### The Dominionistic Attitude

This attitude is oriented toward satisfactions derived from the mastery and control of animals, typically in a sporting context (e.g., rodeos, trophy hunting, bullfighting). Animals are valued largely as challenging opponents, providing opportunities for the display of prowess, skill, strength, and often masculinity. The conquest of the animal demonstrates superiority and dominance—the human ability to confront wildness and render it submissive and orderly. The most valued animals are those viewed as fierce or cunning competitors. The major interest lies in challenge, confrontation, and competition.

### The Negativistic and Neutralistic Attitudes

The fundamental characteristic of the negativistic attitude is an active dislike or fear of animals. In contrast, the neutralistic attitude is more passive, oriented toward avoidance of animals by reason of indifference. Both attitudes share a common sense of alienation or emotional separation from animals. Thus the two perspectives tend to be in agreement that a basic lack in affective and rational capacities distinguishes other animals from humans. Both attitudes evince little sense of kinship or affinity for animals.

## Measuring Attitudes toward Animals

The results presented here are largely based on a national survey of 3,107 randomly selected individuals. Respondents were chosen according to a probability-random-selection method roughly ensuring that every individual in the American population had an equal chance of being selected. A

9

comparison with national census data indicates that the sample was a relatively good cross-section of the American people.

Attitude questionnaires were used to obtain data from which statistical scales were developed to assess the relative distribution of the various attitude types in the American population. Scales were developed for exploratory studies in the mid-1970s (Kellert 1974, 1976). New and more powerful attitude scales were devised for later investigations (Kellert 1978, 1979, 1980a, 1980b). Unfortunately, useful scales could not be developed for either the aesthetic or neutralistic attitudes. (The aesthetic had validity problems, while the neutralistic scale could not be usefully separated from the negativistic. Thus the negativistic scale includes most of the elements of the neutralistic attitude.) Therefore, the results that follow are confined largely to the other eight attitudes.

Sixty-five attitude questions were used in the development of the scales for the national survey. The smallest scale (the ecologistic) consisted of four questions, and the largest (the utilitarian) included thirteen questions. Whenever appropriate, the strength of the response (e.g., strongly versus slightly agree/disagree) was included. Scale scores ranged from 0 to 11 for the ecologistic scale, and from 0 to 27 for the utilitarian. The independence of the scales was partially indicated by relatively small scale intercorrelations, fourteen under 0.20; the smallest was 0.04 (correlating the dominionistic and naturalistic scales); the largest negative correlation was -0.42 (the naturalistic and negativistic attitudes); and the largest positive correlation was 0.40 (the naturalistic and ecologistic).

The scales are admittedly crude approximations of the attitude types, and only in the broadest sense measure their true prevalence and distribution in the American population. Nevertheless, the relative frequency of the attitudes in the national sample of 3,107 respondents was assessed by standardizing the various scale-score distribution frequencies for each attitude, and then using these frequency curves and regression figures to estimate the relative "popularity" of the attitudes. Since particular scores on one attitude scale cannot be equated with similiar scores on other scales, this procedure only roughly indicates the relative frequency of the ten attitudes in the American population. The results of this analysis are summarized in Table 1.

*Table 1.*

## Attitude Occurrence in American Society.

| Attitude | Estimated % of American population strongly oriented toward the attitude* |
|---|---|
| Naturalistic | 10 |
| Ecologistic | 7 |
| Humanistic | 35 |
| Moralistic | 20 |
| Scientistic | 1 |
| Aesthetic | 15 |
| Utilitarian | 20 |
| Dominionistic | 3 |
| Negativistic | 2 |
| Neutralistic | 35 |

*Totals more than 100% as persons can be strongly oriented toward more than one attitude. (Adapted from Kellert 1980b.)

These results suggest that the most common attitudes toward animals in contemporary American society, by a large margin, are the humanistic, moralistic, utilitarian, and negativistic/neutralistic. In many respects, the attitudes can be conceptually subsumed under two broad and conflicting perceptions of animals. Specifically, the moralistic and utilitarian attitudes actively clash around the theme of human exploitation of animals, with the former opposing many exploitative uses of animals involving death and presumed suffering (e.g., hunting, trapping, whaling, laboratory experimentation), while the latter endorses such utilization if significant human benefit results. In somewhat analogous fashion, the negativistic/neutralistic and humanistic attitudes tend to clash with one another, although typically in a more latent manner, around the theme of affection for animals, with the former indifferent and incredulous toward the notion of "loving" animals, while the latter involves intense emotional attachments to animals. The relative popularity of these four attitudes in American society suggests a dynamic basis for the conflict and misunderstanding existing today over various issues involving people and animals.

The scientistic and dominionistic attitudes, according to the results presented in Table 1, are the least common perceptions of animals among the American public. The naturalistic attitude is strongly present among a minority of Americans, but only weakly in evidence among the majority. A substantial number of respondents expressed modest support for the ecologistic viewpoint, but very few were strongly oriented in that direction.

# The Prevalence of Specific Attitudes among Americans

The following analysis examines the prevalence of specific attitudes in various demographic groups. Of particular interest were the attitudes of respondents involved in animal-oriented activity groups.

### The Naturalistic Attitude

The most naturalistic demographic groups included people with graduate-school and college educations, Alaskan and Pacific Coast residents and respondents under thirty-five years of age (see Figures 1, 2, and 3). In contrast, the least naturalistic were respondents with less than a high-school education and persons over fifty-six years of age.

A comparison of this attitude among animal activity groups revealed that nature "hunters" had the highest scores, along with members of environmental-protection organizations (e.g., the Sierra Club, the Wilderness Society), and birders. The naturalistic scores of nature buffs were far higher than those of meat or recreational hunters. Antihunters, livestock raisers, and fisherman had comparatively low scores on this attitude scale, although all animal activity groups had higher scores on the naturalistic scale than did the general population.

12

EDUCATION GROUPS BY SELECTED KNOWLEDGE AND ATTITUDE SCALES

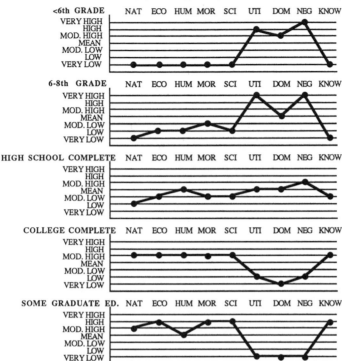

*Figure 1. Attitude profile of demographic groups based on five educational categories. Included at right is the score for general knowledge of animals in each category. The results were derived from attitude scales developed for a national survey of 3,107 people. (Adapted from Kellert 1980b.)*

The Ecologistic Attitude

Demographic results with regard to the ecologistic scale were similiar to those obtained for the naturalistic scale. The most positively related demographic categories were individuals with graduate-school and college education, Alaska residents, persons with professional or managerial occupations, and residents of towns with five hundred to two thousand in population. The lowest-scoring groups included those with less

REGIONS BY SELECTED KNOWLEDGE AND ATTITUDE SCALES

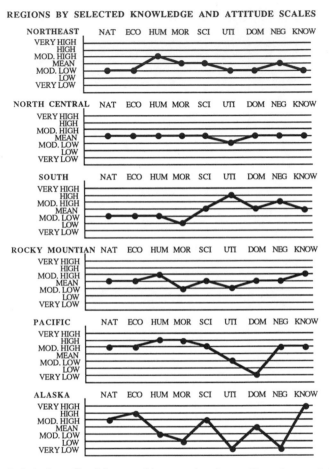

*Figure 2. Attitude profile of demographic groups based on residence in one of six regions of the United States. (Adapted from Kellert 1980b.)*

than a high school education, unskilled blue-collar employees, and the fifty-six through seventy-five age group.

The results of the ecologistic scale among animal activity groups were roughly similiar to those obtained on the naturalistic scale, with the addition of particularly high ecologistic scores among members of wildlife-protection and sportsmen-related organizations and scientific-study hobby-

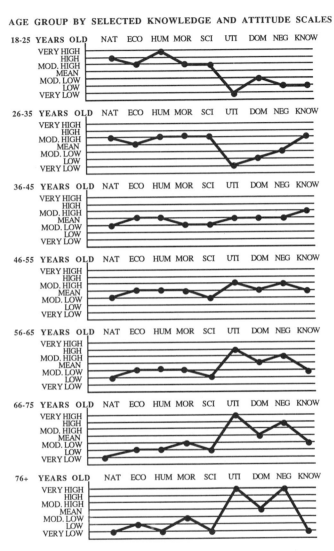

*Figure 3. Attitude profile of demographic groups based on seven age categories. (Adapted from Kellert 1980b.)*

ists. Interestingly, zoo enthusiasts had comparatively low scores on this dimension.

### The Humanistic Attitude

Persons under twenty-five years of age, those earning $20,000–$35,000, and Pacific Coast residents were the most humanistically-oriented demographic groups. In contrast, farmers, persons over seventy-six years of age, and residents of the most rural areas had the lowest scores on this attitude dimension. More females were characterized by this attitude than were males.

Among animal activity groups, humane and environmental-protection-organization members, zoo visitors, antihunters, and scientific-study hobbyists all scored very high on the humanistic scale. In contrast, livestock producers, nature buffs, and, surprisingly, birdwatchers had much lower scores. Apparently these latter groups, in light of their high scores on the naturalistic scale (with the exception of livestock producers), were far more oriented toward wildlife and outdoor recreation values than toward the benefits derived from love of animals, particularly pets.

### The Moralistic Attitude

Those demographic groups expressing the greatest moralistic concern were Pacific Coast residents, the highly educated, those engaged in clerical occupations, females, and respondents under thirty-five years of age. Groups least troubled by animal welfare and cruelty issues were rural residents, farmers, respondents from Alaska and the South, and males.

Animal activity groups scoring high on the moralistic scale included members of humane and environmental-protection organizations and antihunters. Scientific-study hobbyists also had high scores on this dimension. Recreation and meat hunters, sportsmen's organization members, trappers, fishermen, and livestock producers scored very low on this attitude scale.

### The Scientistic Attitude

Among social demographic groups, the highly educated, the young, and Alaska respondents had the highest scientistic scale scores, in marked contrast to the very low scores of the elderly and the poorly educated.

As one might expect, scientific-study hobbyists had the highest scientistic scale scores. Wildlife-protection-organization members and bird-watchers also had relatively high scores. Livestock raisers, fishermen, antihunters, and meat hunters, in contrast, had much lower scores, although all animal activity groups had means above the general population average.

The Utilitarian Attitude

Farmers, the elderly, and Southern respondents had the highest scores on the utilitarian scale. In contrast, persons with a graduate-school education, Alaska respondents, and those under thirty-five years of age indicated the least utilitarian interest in animals (Figures 1, 2, 3). Single persons and residents of areas with a population of one million or more were also characterized by the lowest frequency of the utilitarian attitude.

Among animal activity groups, livestock producers, meat hunters, and fishermen displayed an especially strong utilitarian orientation in contrast to members of humane, wildlife-protection and environmental-protection organizations, and, to a somewhat lesser degree, scientific-study hobbyists, backpackers, and birdwatchers.

The Dominionistic Attitude

Farmers, males, and those with high incomes were the most dominionistically-oriented demographic groups. Females, Pacific Coast respondents, the highly educated, and clerical workers scored lowest on this scale. Differences among the most affluent and educated on the dominionistic scale were in marked contrast to similarities between these higher socioeconomic groups on other attitude scales, and suggested that high income and advanced education do not necessarily result in the same perceptions of animals.

The most dominionistically-oriented animal activity groups were trappers and hunters. Humane-organization members and antihunters had the lowest scores on this attitude scale, suggesting that differences in the dominionistic perception of animals represented a basic and important distinction in the perspectives of hunters and antihunters. Zoo visitors and environmental-protection-organization members also had comparatively low scores on this scale.

The Negativistic Attitude
Among demographic groups, the elderly, those of limited education, and females had the highest negativistic scale scores. In contrast, persons with graduate-school education, Alaska residents, respondents under twenty-five years of age, and those residing in towns or areas with a population under five hundred were the least negativistic in their perception of animals.

No animal activity group revealed marked disinterest in or dislike of animals as measured by the negativistic attitude scale, although livestock producers did score only slightly above the general population mean. Interestingly, antihunters had comparatively high scores on this dimension, suggesting that broad principles concerning the ethical treatment of animals were more salient considerations in opposition to hunting than general interest in animals. Environmental- and wildlife-protection-organization members, scientific-study hobbyists, and birdwatchers were the least negativistic.

## Additional Findings

Attitude profiles of selected demographic groups are provided as an illustration of comparative group variations across all of the attitude dimensions. Educational group differences (Figure 1), for example, indicate that respondents of limited education had considerably lower scores than the highly educated on all the attitude dimensions with the exception of the dominionistic, utilitarian, and negativistic scales. These findings suggest a relative disinterest in and lack of affection for animals among the least educated, with the possible exception of situations involving sporting satisfactions and material gain. Indeed, the dramatic differences among the educational levels pointed to a fundamental divergence in the perceptions of animals and the natural world between those with the least and those with the most education in our society.

Regional differences (Figure 2) were also fairly large and somewhat surprising. One of the most striking results was the stronger wildlife interest, concern, and appreciation of Alaska respondents. In general, the western states revealed greater wildlife appreciation and knowledge, while the South was characterized by the least interest and concern for animals and the most utilitarian orientation.

Age profiles are presented in Figure 3. Differences between the oldest and youngest respondents were especially striking on nearly every attitude dimension, particularly on the naturalistic, humanistic, and utilitarian scales.

# Knowledge of Animals

In the national survey of 3,107 people, members of animal activity groups scored significantly higher on the knowledge of animals scale than did the general public. However, birdwatchers, nature buffs, scientific-study hobbyists, and all types of conservation-related organization members had significantly higher scores than did livestock producers, antihunters, zoo enthusiasts, sport and recreation hunters, and fishermen. Among demographic groups the most knowledgeable were persons with higher education (especially graduate training), Alaska residents, and males. In contrast, the least informed about animals—even after accounting for the interrelationships of all demographic variables—were respondents with less than a high-school education, persons over seventy-five, and, interestingly, under twenty-five years of age, and residents of cities with a population of one million or more.

The American public, as a whole, was characterized by extremely limited knowledge of animals. On questions dealing with endangered species, no more than one-third of the respondents obtained the correct answer; for example, only 26 percent knew the manatee is not an insect, and just 26 percent correctly judged the statement, "The passenger pigeon and the Carolina parakeet are now extinct." Regarding other knowledge questions, just 13 percent knew that raptors are not small rodents, and one half of the sample incorrectly judged the statement, "Spiders have ten legs." A better but still distressingly low 54 percent knew that veal does not come from lamb, and just 57 percent knew that insects do not have backbones. The knowledge questions were divided into a number of generic categories. A comparison of mean scores revealed that the public was most knowledgeable on questions concerning animals implicated in human injury, pets, basic characteristics of animals (e.g., "All adult birds have feathers"), and domestic animals in general. On the other hand, they were least knowledgeable about invertebrates, "taxonomic" distinctions (e.g., "Koala bears are not really bears"), and predators.

## Species Preferences

In the national survey, people were queried on their feelings about thirty-three species ranked on a seven-point like/dislike scale (the most and the least liked are indicated in Table 2). The most preferred were two common

*Figure 4. The most preferred species in a national survey were two domesticated animals—the dog and the horse (Kellert 1980b.)*

*Table 2.*

## Animal Preferences.

| Most Liked Animals | | Least Liked Animals | |
|---|---|---|---|
| *Animal* | *Mean Score** | *Animal* | *Mean Score* |
| Dog | 1.70 | Cockroach | 6.45 |
| Horse | 1.79 | Mosquito | 6.27 |
| Swan | 1.97 | Rat | 6.26 |
| Robin | 1.99 | Wasp | 5.68 |
| Butterfly | 2.04 | Rattlesnake | 5.66 |
| Trout | 2.12 | Bat | 5.35 |
| Salmon | 2.26 | Vulture | 4.91 |
| Eagle | 2.29 | Shark | 4.82 |
| Elephant | 2.63 | Skunk | 4.42 |
| Turtle | 2.69 | Lizard | 4.13 |
| Cat | 2.74 | Crow | 4.06 |
| Ladybug | 2.78 | Coyote | 4.02 |
| Raccoon | 2.80 | Wolf | 3.98 |

*Lower score indicates greater preference. (Adapted from Kellert 1980b.)

domestic animals (the dog and the horse, Figure 4) followed by two familiar and highly aesthetic bird species and an insect (the swan, robin, and butterfly). The trout—a popular and highly attractive game species— was the best-liked fish, and the most preferred wild predator was the eagle. The most favored wild mammal was the elephant.

On the other hand, the two least-liked animals were insect pests (the cockroach and the mosquito, Figure 5). The third, fourth, and fifth least-preferred animals—the rat, wasp, and rattlesnake—have all been implicated in physical injury or disease afflicting human beings. Relatively negative views of the coyote and the wolf were of particular interest given the ongoing controversy over predator-control programs in the United States and the considerable amount of favorable publicity received by the wolf in

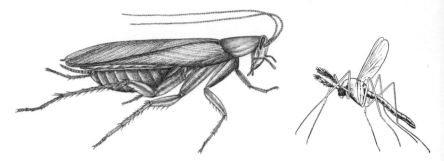

*Figure 5. The two least liked species in a national survey were insect pests—the cockroach and the mosquito (Kellert 1980b). (Cockroach illustration by Vichai Malikul.)*

recent years. High standard-deviation scores for the wolf, coyote, lizard, skunk, vulture, bat, shark, and cat suggested considerable variation in public opinion regarding the positive and negative qualities of these animals.

A qualitative assessment of these results and an examination of related literature (Ehrenfeld 1979, Guggisberg 1970, Ziswiler 1967) suggest a number of particularly important factors in public preference for different species. These factors include:

1. Size (usually, the larger the animal, the more preferred)
2. Aesthetics (considered "attractive")
3. Intelligence (thought to not only have the capacity for reason but also for feeling and emotion)
4. Danger to Humans
5. Likelihood of Inflicting Property Damage
6. Predatory Tendencies
7. Phylogenetic Relatedness to Humans
8. Cultural and Historical Relationship to Humans
9. Relationship to Human Society (pet, domestic farm animal, game, pest, native wildlife, exotic wildlife)
10. Texture (bodily appearance and structure; generally, the more unfamiliar to humans, the less preferred)

11. Mode of Locomotion (generally, the more unfamiliar to humans, the less preferred)

12. Economic Value of the Species to Humans

# Conclusion

A variety of results have been presented suggesting considerable public interest in and affection for animals. On the other hand, a great deal of variation and conflict was found in the attitudes, perceptions, and knowledge of animals among diverse groups in American society. While a bedrock of affection and concern was found, it appears that much needs to happen before this appreciative orientation is usefully broadened to encompass a more biologically knowledgeable and ethically sensitive feeling for animals. Those responsible for animal welfare and natural environments should recognize this public sympathy for and interest in animals and devote increasing efforts to addressing the needs for greater awareness and understanding. The challenges are great for wildlife professionals, humane educators, natural-resource managers, and others responsible for the future wellbeing of the nonhuman world. Until these human variables are more deeply understood, however, it is doubtful that the erosion of land resources and the destruction of fauna can be arrested.

# Select Bibliography

Ehrenfeld, D.W. 1970. *Biological conservation.* New York: Holt.

Guggisberg, C.A.W. 1970. *Man and wildlife.* New York: Arco Publishing Co.

Kellert, S.R. 1974. *From kinship to mastery: A study of American attitudes toward animals.* A report to the U.S. Fish and Wildlife Service. Yale University.

———. 1976. Perceptions of animals in American society. *Transactions of the 41st North American Wildlife and Natural Resources Conference,* pp. 533–46. Washington, D.C.: Wildlife Management Office.

———. 1978. *Policy implications of a national study of American attitudes and behavioral relations with animals.* U.S. Fish and Wildlife Service, U.S. Department of the Interior. Washington, D.C.: U.S. Government Printing Office.

————. 1979. *Public attitudes toward critical wildlife and natural habitat issues: Phase I.* U.S. Fish and Wildlife Service, U.S. Department of the Interior. Washington, D.C.: U.S. Government Printing Office.

————. 1980a. Contemporary values of wildlife in American society. In *Wildlife values,* ed. W.W. Shaw and E.H. Zube. U.S. Forest Service, Rocky Mountain Forest and Range Experiment Station, Institutional Series, Report #1.

————. 1980b. American attitudes toward and knowledge of animals: An update. *International Journal for the Study of Animal Behavior* 1:87–119.

————. 1984. Urban American perceptions and uses of animals and the natural environment. *Urban Ecology* 8:209–228.

————. 1985. Socioeconomic factors in endangered species management. *Journal of Wildlife Management* 49:528–36.

Pomerantz, G.A. 1977. *Young peoples' attitudes toward wildlife.* Wildlife Division Report #2781. Michigan Department of Natural Resources.

Westervelt, M.O., and L.G. Llewellyn. 1986. Interests and educational needs of young people relating to wildlife. Paper presented at the 1st National Symposium on Social Science and Resource Management. Oregon State University, Corvallis, May 1986.

Ziswiler, V. 1967 *Extinct and vanishing animals.* London: The English Universities Press.

# Changing Perceptions
# of Animals:
# A Philosophical View

**Lilly-Marlene Russow**

An examination of attitudes in American society over the past one hundred fifty years reveals that animals have been perceived as everything from resources to be exploited—literally, sources of horsepower—to incarnations of grace and beauty, fit subjects for works of art. Native wildlife usually has been perceived as a source of food, clothing, and shelter. The most prominent example is the American bison, which provided the Plains Indians with meat and hides. But along with this attitude can also be found—one hundred fifty years ago as well as today—a different perception: wildlife as a national treasure to be preserved, protected, and admired on its own terms. This duality of attitude is also apparent in our feelings toward domestic animals raised for food and toward our companion animals, the cats and dogs that share our homes.

# Relevant Philosophical Concepts

Before we can assess these different ways of perceiving animals, and before we can ask how we *ought* to perceive them, we must first get a better understanding of what these diverse attitudes are. In order to do this, I would like to introduce a concept provided by the twentieth-century German philosopher, Martin Heidegger. In his best-known work, *Being and Time*, written in 1927, Heidegger developed a distinction between seeing things as "ready-to-hand," that is, being available as a tools or equipment (usable things), and seeing them as "present-at-hand"—as physical objects which are simply there or merely present, but have no immediate purpose. Henceforth, to avoid confusion, the concept of present-at-hand will be referred to as "simply there." This distinction between "ready-to-hand" and "simply there" can help us understand the shift in society's attitudes toward animals.

The model that Heidegger uses for grasping something as "ready-to-hand" is our use of a tool, such as a hammer. We do not have to look at the hammer objectively and disinterestedly: We grasp its essential nature by using it. This form of understanding is preconceptual: We do not theorize about hammers, or categorize them, but we manage to understand them anyway. They are part of the world that we move through, rather than the laboratory world that we look *at*. We can summarize all of this by saying that when something is "ready-to-hand" for us, we are seeing it only as a piece of equipment which serves a specific purpose for us.

However, sometimes hammers break, and we have to adopt a different attitude toward them, or sometimes we are not engaged in hammering, but are simply observing the objects around us. When we look at something objectively, scientifically, and disinterestedly, that thing becomes "simply there" for us. This means that I begin to impose concepts on it by describing it and classifying it, and I also begin to be more conscious of the separation of subject from object—that is, of the fact that I am distinct from it, in contrast with the "ready-to-hand" hammer that is almost part of me, an extension of my hand. Since they are not an extension of me, I can have an objective, theoretical attitude toward objects that are "simply there" in my world.

One of the important features of these distinctions is that things can shift back and forth between the two modes: Something that is now "ready-to-hand" for me can become "simply there," and vice versa. I would like to suggest that one of the most striking features about our changing perception of animals in the past one hundred fifty years is a movement from a predominantly "ready-to-hand" attitude to one that regards animals as "simply there" (Figure 1). This chapter will explore the reasons for and the results of this shift. Nonetheless, one must also recognize a normative element in this analysis, a question of whether the shift from "ready-to-hand" to "simply there" has led to more accurate perception of animals. As the following account will suggest, the results are mixed.

Perceiving something as "ready-to-hand" does not require that we understand it intuitively, but only that we understand those aspects of it that are relevant to our interaction: A farmer must have an accurate understanding of his animals' needs insofar as they affect the beasts' health and growth, but no further. A "simply there" mode of understanding is more open, and thus allows room for more depth and breadth, but unlike "ready-to-hand" interactions, it lacks the touchstone of "getting the job done." As a result, there is a potential not only for deep appreciation but also for significant misperception of animals.

## Factors Affecting Attitudes

If we survey the factors that affect our attitudes towards animals, they fall into roughly three categories: historical circumstances, emotional orientation, and intellectual climate. *Historical circumstances* comprise the way people live: where and how they live, the way work is done, and the way people function in the world. *Emotional orientation* can be thought of as what are sometimes referred to as "instinctive reactions" but are actually learned ways of responding—molded by society's influence in the form of

*Figure 1. A century ago, when Americans lived primarily in rural settings, animals were an essential part of their daily lives; animals were tools, "ready-to-hand," to help people survive. Today, few Americans are dependent on animals for their liveli-hood; animals, especially wild ones, are frequently perceived as national treasures to be preserved, protected, and admired. (Illustration by Sally Bensusen.)*

standards of expected behavior, popular literature, and other forms of social influence that are more subtle and indirect. The *intellectual climate* is determined by the philosophers, scientists, and other theorists and intellectuals of the day. Although emotional orientation and intelletual climate often coincide, intellectual climate depends more on reason and argument than does emotional orientation, which depends more on a subconscious influence on attitudes.

## Historical Circumstances

Let us begin with a closer look at historical circumstances, for as we shall see, these set the stage for the influence of the other two sorts of factors. If we take a broad overview of American history since 1830, the most striking factors seem to be: (1) the move from a primarily rural society to one in which the vast majority of people live in cities; (2) the Civil War and the abolition of slavery; (3) industrialization, along with the rise and fall of child labor; and (4) the two World Wars, each of which tended to move men onto battlefields and women into factories and other jobs outside the home. The last three factors affected our perceptions of animals indirectly through their influence on emotional orientation and intellectual climate. Before that, however, urbanization had a direct impact on the way in which people interacted with animals.

In a predominantly rural setting, animals are all around, "ready-to-hand." They are beasts of burden and the source of meat, hide, wool, eggs, and milk; they are part of the equipment with which the farm family ekes out an existence. Wildlife, too, is seen as "ready-to-hand": Animals are hunted and trapped for food and clothing and as salable commodities. It is important to remember, though, that perceiving something as "ready-to-hand" does involve a deep understanding, although it is a practical rather than a theoretical one. Someone who encounters animals as "ready-to-hand" must combine exploitation with understanding. A person for whom a beaver or horse is a source of fur or locomotion must understand a great deal about the beaver or horse in order to use it effectively.

When people moved to the city, their opportunities to relate to animals changed dramatically. Animals were still all around, of course,

*Figure 2. Domesticated pigs. In the nineteenth century many farm animals were still to be found within city limits. In 1842 it was reported that as many as ten thousand pigs were located in New York City (Duffy 1968).*

especially in the ninetenth century. Herds of pigs were prevalent in the largest cities (Figure 2), and cattle were commonly driven through the streets. It has been estimated that ten thousand pigs lived within the city limits of New York in 1842 (Duffy 1968), and several incidents involving runaway cows were reported in New York as late as 1889 (Carson 1972). But these animals were owned and tended by only a few people, while the majority of the urban population had to confront animals as something to deal with, a new problem to understand and solve. Just as a hammer which breaks becomes "simply there," so too did animals in an urban setting shift toward being perceived as "simply there."

This is especially true of horses. Although they remained the main source of power for urban transportation well into the twentieth century, fewer and fewer people owned their own horses, and more and more relied on hired cabs, wagons, and omnibuses. The fact that these changes caused people to look directly at animals, and to try to understand them in ways other than as tools, is reflected in the fact that the first humane legislation and animal-welfare movements had the treatment of cattle and horses as their primary targets.

In England, for example, Colonel Richard Martin, also known as "Humanity Dick" Martin, was the foremost crusader for animal-welfare legislation, with a primary emphasis on cattle and horses. In fact, a bill known as "An Act to Prevent the Cruel and Improper Treatment of Cattle," which was passed by Parliament in 1822 largely due to Martin's efforts, was the first legislation which made cruelty itself, rather than malice toward an animal's owner, a legal offense (Carson 1972).

In America, the situation was similar. Henry Bergh, the founder of the American Society for the Prevention of Cruelty to Animals (ASPCA), was especially dedicated to the protection of cart horses. His campaign led to significant improvement in the treatment of horses in the 1860s, once again with a primary emphasis on the treatment of the urban horse population.

As animals of this sort began to fade from the urban environment in the twentieth century, Americans began to witness a marked increase in the number of pets being kept (Figure 3). To speculate on this as evidence of a human need for contact with animals would go beyond the scope of this discussion, but it is interesting to compare this phenomenon with one noted by some present-day animal scientists: Farmers who practice intensive livestock operations, which result in a lessening of individual contact between the farmer and his animals, are more likely to keep pets than farmers using more traditional methods. In any event, as people began to confront dogs and cats as "simply there" rather than as instruments for hunting, herding, or catching mice, their perceptions changed.

The situation that arises when the perception of something as "ready-to-hand" is abandoned or disrupted is a difficult one. When we encounter something as "simply there," we still must understand it *as something;* we need a set of concepts or categories with which to interpret and describe it, and we require a model or theory to help guide our understanding. Historical circumstances disrupted the situation in which most people encountered animals as "ready-to-hand," leaving a gap to be filled by new ways of perceiving animals. This gap was gradually filled by the other two factors, the emotional orientation and the intellectual climate.

*Figure 3. In the 1900s farm animals began to disappear from ever-growing urban areas. At the same time city dwellers increasingly began to keep pets. This change reflected a shift from a utilitarian perception to a more personal attachment to animals. (Illustration by Richard Swartz.)*

## Emotional Orientation

The emotional orientation that has been fostered in the past one hundred fifty years is, not surprisingly, a complex and ambivalent one. As people began to concentrate in cities, animals became, among other things, a spectacle: things to be wondered at, amused by, or gawked at. In the late 1800s, zoos and circuses became popular, offering strange animals to be ogled, not understood. People learned to perceive animals as exotic and alien phenomena.

With the growth of the humane movement, though, other elements were introduced. A group affiliated with the Massachusetts SPCA sponsored the first paperback edition of Anna Sewell's *Black Beauty* (Carson 1972), which was one of many children's books that portrayed animals in a highly anthropomorphic way. Victorian moralizing was combined with sentimentality to produce an extremely strong feeling of outrage against blatant mistreatment of animals.

Another important factor in the changing emotional orientation toward animals over the past one hundred fifty years was the "romance of the wild." The development of the American West gave rise to conflicting images, one of which was the myth of the "noble savage" who lived in harmony with all of nature, using animals for his needs but understanding them deeply as well. This romantic image can be found in one form or another in many nineteenth-century writings as well as in some nature films of today, where, for example, the wolf is portrayed as a benevolent guardian of the health of deer herds, and the natural life of animals is portrayed as idyllic.

Perhaps the most interesting aspect of American culture's emotional orientation toward animals is the tendency to *neotenize* them, to see them as children—an attitude which combines many of the elements discussed so far. Suppose one entertains a romantic vision of the wild as unspoiled innocence, of animals as the proper subject of sentimental concern, yet still holds that adult humans have some sort of responsibility toward them, tied to our more developed rationality. Combining all of these feelings creates a picture of animals as innocent children: cute and unspoiled, but in need of protection by more rational beings—us. This view of animals as infantile is still quite prevalent, and can be found, for example, in children's literature about animals, and especially in literature dealing with our responsilbilities toward wildlife. This neotenization is a mixed blessing: Animals perceived in this way are more likely to elicit a positive emotional response and perhaps even protection, but it also implies helplessness and lack of autonomy. Animals need *us* to be able to cope—but the possibility of self-actualization is denied to anything seen as lacking autonomy.

Most of the emotional factors which have shaped our perception of animals support an increased concern for animal welfare and animal rights. However, this orientation is a two-edged sword, in that the concern is often misinformed by a mythic picture of animals rather than an accurate understanding of them on their own terms.

## Intellectual Climate

It is in the intellectual climate, though, that factors influencing our changing perception of animals are the most far-reaching and influential. From this standpoint it should be noted that at the beginning of the nineteenth century, the Age of Reason still reigned. Reason was seen as a faculty not only uniquely human but man's greatest achievement, which set him apart from mere beasts. The movement away from this starting point is one of the two salient features of the intellectual climate of the past one hundred fifty years, the other being an increased attention to the concept of basic human rights.

The idea that reason was a unique and important feature of humanity can be traced back to Plato and Aristotle in ancient Greece, but it was given its most forceful modern formulation by the philosopher-mathematician René Descartes in the seventeenth century. He argued that only human beings possess souls and are capable of reason. Although Descartes lived and wrote well before the one-hundred-fifty-year period that is the focus of my argument, his influence, which is still prevalent, had an enormous impact on a philosopher whose work did usher in the nineteenth century, Immanuel Kant. It was Kant who bound reason and morality so closely together, and argued that because animals lack the capacity to reason in

34

ways that would allow them to act autonomously—not merely in response to instinct and need—we can have no moral duties toward them. Any ethical limitations on the way we treat animals reflect indirect duties to other humans: We may not injure another person's cattle because that would be a failure to respect his property rights, and we should discourage cruelty to animals when it might lead to cruelty toward other people. Most of Kant's conclusions regarding our treatment of animals were echoes of the position defended by Thomas Aquinas centuries earlier, but Kant's reiteration of them ensured they would receive due consideration by the intellectual leaders of the nineteenth century.

We can discern three features of Kant's moral philosophy that are particularly important in shaping perceptions of animals. First, the basic premise is that human reason is the ultimate guide for human action; animals, lacking reason, operate on a very different plane, being moved about by the irrational forces of instinct. Second, Kant explicitly saw morality as bound to rationality: One had to be a rational agent in order to be a proper subject for moral concern. This is crucial because it relegates concerns for animal welfare to the level of misguided sentimentality rather than informed ethical judgment. Finally, Kant offered the criterion of human benefit as a way of determining the legitimacy of legislation or moral strictures governing the treatment of animals. Taking the latter two points together, we find in the nineteenth and early twentieth centuries that humane legislation was often given "rational" justification in terms of benefits to humans, while concerns that did not meet these criteria, such as the antivivisectionist movement, were taken much less seriously.

This entire Kantian edifice was shaken and irrevocable weakened by the major scientific revolution of the nineteenth century that resulted from the general acceptance of Darwin's theory of evolution. By breaking down the barriers between man and the rest of the animal kingdom, Darwin cast doubt on the idea that there was a clear dividing line between reason and instinct, between the forces that shape our behavior and those that guide animals. Although his ideas were, and sometimes still are, met with resistance and ridicule, it gradually became less and less plausible to act on the assumption that there exists an unbridgeable chasm between animals and humans. As the assumption became discredited, so too did the moral arguments based on them; it became possible to entertain the hypothesis that some duties might be owed directly to animals—that they, too, might have rights. This brings us to the second feature of the changing intellectual climate I wish to examine.

Talk of "human rights," of course, antedates the nineteenth century; it found its most dramatic expression in the American and French Revolutions of the previous century. However, these rights were for the most part *negative* rights—the right to be free from certain kinds of threats, harm, or coercion—and they were usually seen as applying to adult white males. This latter fact is part of the influences of Kantian reason, with adults being considered more rational than children, men more rational than women, and whites more rational than blacks or Indians.

In the nineteenth and twentieth centuries, the conception of rights, and right-holders, expanded dramatically. Historical circumstances motivated this expansion, and thus effected important changes in the intellectual understanding of rights. The abolition of slavery and the civil rights movement gradually broke down racial barriers. The brutal exploitation of children in factories eventually triggered a revolt against such treatment, bringing with it a realization that children, too, might be considered in terms of their own rights and interests, not merely as objects of their parents' plans. Women winning the right to vote, gaining increased opportunities for higher education, and becoming more and more important contributors to the work force were the inevitable consequences of increased attention to the rights of women. Each expansion of the sphere of rights set the stage for the next movement, as arguments for one case were applied to others. Mary Wollstonecraft's treatise, *A Vindication of the Rights of Women*, was parodied by an anonymous *Vindication of the Rights of Animals* (Singer 1974). Although the latter was originally an attempt to show the absurdity of recognizing women's rights, the parallel was turned upside down by those who argued for both sorts of rights. Peter Singer is a recent example of this: In *Animal Liberation* (1977) he explicitly bases his argument against "speciesism" on more traditional rejections of racism and sexism.

This expansion of human rights forced moral philosophers to examine the whole concept of rights more carefully. Thus, particularly in the twentieth century, rights became more closely tied to individuals' interests, and less to some exalted and mysterious force of reason. This in turn contributed to arguments for animal rights. Even if animals lack the capacity for complex abstract thought, they clearly have interests that can be recognized and respected.

Moreover, this new attention to human and animal rights was accompanied by a shift in the nature of the rights themselves. Even a cursory examination of changes in legislation and judicial procedures reveals that, while at the beginning of the nineteenth century rights were primarily a form of protection against certain sorts of treatment, this was gradually supplemented with a more positive view of "welfare rights," in which a subject was seen to have a right to certain basic requirements for a good life. The general acceptance of the idea of a right to adequate food, shelter, and other positive goods is a contemporary phenomenon.

One final change in the intellectual climate must be mentioned in conjunction with our changing perception of animals. Within the scientific community, scientists have become more "professional" in the past one hundred fifty years. People who work, as Darwin did, outside an academic setting and without proper quantitative procedures are now considered talented amateurs rather than real scientists. In science generally, but particularly in those sciences which deal with our understanding of animals, anecdotal evidence and speculative anthropomorphic theorizing based on our own behavior and needs have been abandoned in favor of more carefully controlled, quantitative, and objective research. We are even beginning to develop objective and scientifically acceptable methods for dealing with such "unscientific" factors as the intelligence, interests, feelings, and desires of animals.

## Summary and Conclusions

My analysis can be summarized by noting that historical circumstances during the past one hundred fifty years forced a general change from perceiving animals as "ready-to-hand" (available as a tool or a usable thing) to perceiving them as "simply there." Certainly a "ready-to-hand" orientation requires a great deal of understanding of animals on their own terms, but a more critical look reveals that this attitude has no room for the animal as autonomous being with its own goals, interests, and world. For that reason, a shift to seeing animals as "simply there" offers at least the opportunity to develop a richer and better-balanced perception. However, the categories and models by which animals are understood in this new mode are left open, and hence are continuously subject to the flux of emotional orientation and intellectual climate.

Changes in the intellectual climate did much to shape our changing perception of animals. Reason had been, but can no longer be, viewed as a clear and distinct dividing line between humans and animals. The concept of rights was reexamined both in its extension to human groups formerly excluded and in its inclusion within "positive" animal welfare right proposals. As a result, there has been a weakening of the connection between rights and rationality. And finally, there is now a more neutral objective attitude used in the attempt to understand animals scientifically.

If we can manage to integrate these changes and diverse influences into a coherent and complete picture, we may yet learn to perceive animals as we ought to: as they really are, rather than as we would have them be, or as we would like to be ourselves.

# Select Bibliography

Carson, G. 1972. *Men, beasts and gods: A history of cruelty and kindness to animals.* New York: Scribners.

Descartes, R. 1973. "Discourse on method," *The philosophical works of Descartes,* trans. E.B.S. Haldane and G.R.T. Ross. New York: Cambridge University Press, pp. 79–130.

Duffy, J. 1968. *A History of public health in New York City.* New York: Russell Sage Foundation.

Heidegger, M. 1927. *Being and time,* trans. J. Macquarrie and E. Robinson. New York: Harper and Row.

Kant, I. 1963. *Lectures on ethics,* trans. L. Infeld. New York: Harper and Row.

Singer, P. 1974. All animals are equal. *Philosophical Exchange*, vol. 1, no. 5. Reprinted 1976. In *Animal rights and human obligations*, ed. T. Regan and P. Singer. Englewood Cliffs: Prentice-Hall.

Singer, P. 1977. *Animal liberation.* New York: Avon Books.

# Anthropomorphism Is Not
# a Four-letter Word

**Randall Lockwood**

When I first entered the world of the scientific study of animal behavior about twenty years ago, I got the distinct impression that it was time to put away my teddy bears and memories of Disney films and acquire the cold, hard stare of the "objective" scientist. I recently went back to my first textbooks in the field to find the phrases that had given me that impression. Here is one of them:

> We cannot see into the animal's mind any more than we can see into that of any of our fellow humans, but that doesn't prevent us in both cases from thinking that we can. The animal may seem sad or happy, but we cannot infer that this is the case from the way that we ourselves might

feel in the same situation. To do so is to indulge in anthropomorphism—
seeing man's shape in all things—and this is the *cardinal crime* for the
animal observer (emphasis added). (Broadhurst 1963:12)

Here is a line from another of my textbooks from my formative years:
"Sometimes we fall into the *dangerous pit* of anthropomorphism (which
means literally 'formed like a man') or the tendency to think of animals as
if they were human" (emphasis added) (Breland and Breland 1966:3).

I would like to spend a little time reviewing why we have been
trained to see this process as bad and why we nonetheless persist in
thinking in anthropomorphic terms. I hope to be able to give you some
idea of how an anthropomorphic perspective can be applied in ways that
are a service to both science and the animals themselves.

# A Brief History of Anthropomorphism in Science

Early accounts of natural history were not only anthropomorphic, they
were anthropocentric. Animals were seen as existing only for man's
benefit or to provide him with some moral lesson about the power and
potential wrath of God or gods. Early accounts were filled with stories
that were anecdotal, anthropomorphic, and largely erroneous.

Throughout the early history of biology there were many compendia
of anthropomorphic anecdotes. Even though the accuracy of the accounts
steadily improved, the frequency of errors made it difficult to equate the
study of animal behavior with the hard and fast quantitative sciences such
as physics, chemistry, and astronomy that were experiencing explosive
growth in the nineteenth century.

Charles Darwin made wide but careful use of anecdotal reports in
many of his greatest works. His descriptions of behavior were also highly
anthropomorphic. He wrote, for example:

Dogs also exhibit their affection by desiring to rub against their masters. . . . I have also seen dogs licking cats with whom they were friends.
This habit probably originated in the females carefully licking their

puppies—the clearest object of their love—for the sake of cleansing them. (Darwin 1872:118)

This was in part a literary convention, and we must remember that he was a best-selling author—the first edition of *On the Origin of Species* sold out in a single day. But Darwin's anthropomorphism also reflected his firm belief in the continuity of all life, including a continuity of mental experience.

# The Rejection of Anthropomorphism

Many of Darwin's contemporaries, eager to join the ranks of the "legitimate" scientists, were critical of this approach, and *The Expression of the Emotions in Man and Animals*, published by Darwin in 1872, was largely ignored by the scientific community for many years. Twenty-two years later, C. Lloyd Morgan released his *Introduction to Comparative Psychology* (1894:53), which contained a simple statement on method that was seized upon by American biologists and psychologists as their guiding light. This principle, now immortalized as "Morgan's Canon," was brief and deceptively simple. He wrote, "In no case may we interpret an action as the outcome of the exercise of a higher psychical faculty if it can be interpreted as the outcome of the exercise of one that stands lower in the psychological scale."

We will explore the implications of this in a moment, but it was generally interpreted to mean, "Don't talk about intelligence when instinct will do; don't discuss 'mind' when 'reflex' will suffice." Like many statements in science that have been zealously embraced, Morgan's Canon had the effect of both freeing animal psychology from many of its pseudoscientific trappings and, at the same time, slamming the door on some of the most interesting questions possible.

Most of the prominent figures in the study of animal behavior from 1890 to the 1950s embraced Morgan's idea. Pavlov (1960 edition:16) wrote that animals should be studied as "physiological facts, without any need to resort to fantastic speculations as to the existence of any possible

43

subjective states . . . which may be conjectured as an analogy with ourselves." In America, John B. Watson (1924:5) set the tone for animal research here for the next forty years when he proclaimed the official position of Behaviorism: " 'States of Consciousness,' like the so-called phenomena of spiritualism are not objectively verifiable and for that reason can *never* become data for science [emphasis added]."

As some people have described it, this is the point where psychology, having lost its *soul*, proceeded to lose its *mind*. Given the choice between accepting the concepts of mind, feeling, and emotions in man and animals alike and seeing how well they worked as sources of hypotheses, or simply denying the possibility of their importance, most chose the latter course.

There are problems with Morgan's Canon and the approaches that followed it. It is unclear just what we are being saved from by adopting it: It is unclear what the actual danger of an anthropomorphic approach might be. The implication is that anthropomorphism is bad science. What does that mean? A primary purpose of the scientific method is to enable us to make valid predictions about the world. The better our science, the better the predictions we are able to make. If anthropomorphism is bad science, then the hypotheses we generate based on assuming things like animal emotion, feeling, or intelligence will tend to be very inaccurate. But Morgan's Canon, Pavlov's view, and Behaviorism tell us not to even bother asking the question! To them, a scientific study of animal emotion or animal suffering or animal consciousness is a contradiction in terms, like a scientific study of the soul. I find it very hard to accept as scientific any philosophy that automatically excludes a particular line of inquiry.

What we got from Morgan, Pavlov, Loeb, Watson, Skinner, and others, who avoided anything that smacked of anthropomorphism, often took the form of precisely measured studies of trivial events. There has been, and continues to be, a fascination with studying areas of animal behavior that lend themselves to precise, objective measurement; not so much because these events are intrinsically interesting or important, but simply because they *can* be measured. The result has often been the expensive measurement of the irrelevant or the painful elaboration of the obvious.

In the 1940s and 1950s, while American psychologists followed a largely Behaviorist tradition, ethologists in Europe were rediscovering many of the Darwinian traditions. Konrad Lorenz, Niko Tinbergen, and others performed both naturalistic observations and natural experiments, in general accord with scientific method. However, they felt free to discuss their results with reference to animals' minds and feelings. As with Darwin, part of this was for popular effect, and, like *On the Origin of Species*, Lorenz's books *On Aggression* and *King Solomon's Ring* became best-sellers. But the intimate anthropomorphic tone also reflected a very different philosophical orientation, one that had been neglected for some time in this country. As Lorenz (1952:152) put it, "Believe me, I am not mistakenly assigning human properties to animals; on the contrary, I am showing you what an enormous inheritance remains in man to this day."

Ironically, one outgrowth of ethology's popularity in the 1960s and 1970s was the proliferation of "zoomorphism," the widespread application of concepts of animal behavior to human motivation and behavior. This has been followed by the more systematic application of principles of Darwinian fitness to human and non-human behavior by contemporary sociobiologists, who can be comfortable freely interchanging terms drawn from studies of both human and animal behavior.

It is important at this point to clarify some of the different meanings that the term *anthropomorphism* has taken on. We have rapidly covered many years of intellectual history here, and clearly the idea has had different meanings at different stages.

## Five Categories of Anthropomorphism

I find it useful to think in terms of five different kinds of anthropomorphism. The first I would call *allegorical anthropomorphism*. This would apply to descriptions of animal behavior that are not intended to be interpreted as biological fact. These descriptions use animals to make an argument more appealing or to conceal true identities. This would be the form of anthropomorphism we see in most fables, Disney films, and literary or political allegories such as *Alice in Wonderland, Animal Farm,* and *Watership Down*. This form is certainly entertaining, and, since it

*Figure 1. People who dress their pets in human clothes fall into the category of anthropomorphism called "personification." Such pet owners typically ignore or do not recognize their pets' true biological needs and adaptations. Dressed-up animals indicate a personal need or statement of the pet owner rather than any requirement that an animal may have. (Illustration by Sally Bensusen.)*

does not presume to portray biological reality, it is essentially harmless. The dangers lie in extending the allegory to the other forms of anthropomorphism below.

The second category, *personification*, is closest to what is commonly thought of as anthropomorphism. Contained in this category are instances of people who dress up their pets in human clothes (Figure 1) and in other ways superimpose their own desires on animals. This is similiar to allegorical anthropomorphism, in that there is no recognition of the true biological needs and adaptations of the animals involved. In this case, however, the animals that are used to portray some personal, symbolic message are not literary figures—they are flesh and blood beings who may suffer in the process.

The third variety is *superficial anthropomorphism*. In this case we are inclined to interpret an animal's behavior or temperament on the basis of surface qualities that are unrelated to those that actually regulate it. For example, we might interpret the "kissing" of such tropical fish as gouramis to indicate affection (Figure 2) because it bears a superficial resemblance to the human pattern, or we may assume the wide-eyed, alert gaze of the owl to reveal unusual intelligence (Figure 3). Such anthropomorphism is bad science since it would lead us to make false predictions. A particularly famous example of this occurs in the recent film "The Right Stuff" where Ham, a chimpanzee, returns from his space flight and greets those who open his capsule with a big toothy grin, which then adorns the cover of *LIFE* magazine. The interpretation of this "smile" was that he had loved his flight. In truth he was simply giving the "fear grimace" that usually accompanies an unsettling chimpanzee experience. But it *looked*

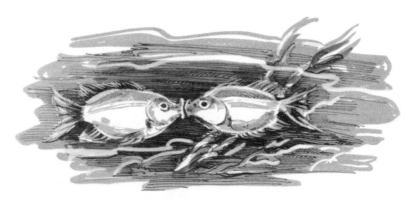

*Figure 2. "Kissing" gouramis. The behavior of these tropical fish has been interpreted as an example of affection in an animal species because the behavior resembles a human pattern. (Illustration by Richard Swartz.)*

*Figure 3. The horned owl. The wide-eyed, alert gaze of the owl has been perceived by humans as suggesting great wisdom and intelligence. (Illustration by Richard Swartz.)*

like a nice big smile. Again, more careful attention to what preceded and followed this behavior could have led to a more accurate interpretation.

A fourth variety is *explanatory anthropomorphism*. With this approach, we are inclined to offer circular definitions and explanations of animal behavior, thinking that by naming a behavior we have explained its basis. For example, a dog owner leaves one dog behind and takes another for a walk and upon his return finds the garbage strewn around the living room. The owner attributes the behavior to "spite" or "revenge" on the part of the dog left behind. How do we recognize it as spite?—because the behavior seemed spiteful! Unfortunately it is not only nonscientists who fall into the trap of thinking things are explained because they are named; human psychiatry has a long history of similiar fallacies.

All of these varieties have shortcomings as tools for science. They either make no attempt to understand the animal in its own world, or they make no attempt to verify that our explanation of a behavior is correct. Since my title suggests that I consider some anthropomorphism to be a potential benefit to science and the animals it studies, this brings me to the form of anthropomorphism I hinted at when describing the works of Darwin and the modern ethologists. This I call *applied anthropomorphism:* the use of our own personal perspective on what it's like to be a living being to suggest ideas about what it is like to be some other being of either our own or some other species. This process is a form of projection, and it is a process that makes our life on earth as social beings possible. Our basic problem is that we cannot get inside someone or something else. I have no immediate way of knowing what it's like to be one of my friends, my wife, the president of the United States, my cat, a wolf, a panda, or a fly on the wall. But the essence of consciousness is using self-knowledge to predict the behavior of others. Like most humans, I can generate hypotheses about what it might be like to be someone or something else and make predictions on the basis of these hypotheses. If I am successful in projecting my experiences on to situations faced by others, my predictions will be accurate. If I fail, then I must reevaluate my hypotheses. This kind of empathic introspection was implied in the writings of Darwin and was elegantly summed up in an early text on animal behavior by Margaret F. Washburn (1917:24):

When a being whose structure resembles ours receives the same stimulus that affects us and moves in the same way as a result, he has an inner experience which resembles our own . . . . We may extend this inference to the lower animals, with proper safeguards, just as far as they present resemblances in structure and behavior to ourselves.

We have to keep two things in mind when applying this idea. First, our projection of our own mental events is only a hypothesis. To be a sound scientific hypothesis it must be falsifiable: There must be some data that could be collected that, depending on the outcome, could lead us to fall back on Morgan's Canon and accept the fact that the individual's mental experiences are different from our own. Such an experiment might be quite complex, or it might be as simple as allowing the animal a choice between two different situations. Second, we must keep in mind the "proper safeguards" alluded to by Washburn.

# Constructive Use of Anthropomorphism

Let us look at these safeguards in some detail. For the entire process to be of any value, we must have analogs of the experience of others in our own repertoire. If I enjoy some book about nature then I can predict with some certainty that a friend who has exhibited a parallel interest will appreciate the book. However, it would probably be erroneous for me to approach a mother who has just buried a child and say, "I know how you must feel." I have known grief, but I doubt that my experiences have given me a pattern analogous to what this mother is experiencing, so I cannot be sure how that person will respond to being left alone, comforted, and so forth. A similar problem arises in dealing with animals. Niko Tinbergen recognized his inability to relate to the experience of incubation on the part of a herring gull. He described the event as ". . . monotonous, at least for the observer, who, missing any incubation instinct in himself, has some difficulty in understanding the satisfaction which a bird presumably feels when just sitting on eggs" (Tinbergen 1953:134).

How are we to judge when there is the potential for analogs of our experience in another species? One powerful source is the study of the physiological substrates of these experiences. As we gain increasing understanding of the anatomical, neurophysiological, and pharmacological events that underlie human emotional states, we are constantly forced to realize the extent of parallels to these events in a wide variety of diverse animals. The neurotransmitters and other biological elements linked to such human experiences as pain, depression, stress, and anxiety are remarkably widespread in the animal world.

50

A second safeguard to which we should pay attention is the context in which a behavior occurs. When dealing with other people we find that our projections tend to fail when we do not know the events that preceded the behavior we are trying to understand. Anthropomorphism fails under similar circumstances, as when we are insensitive to the biology, ecology, or evolutionary history of the animal, as well as to its individual life history. When my colleagues and I released a pack of captive-raised wolves into the Alaskan wilderness, many people suggested that they would be out of sight in a flash, able at last to follow the primordial drive for space and freedom. In fact, the animals returned each night for nearly a week to the temporary cage in which they had been allowed to recover from their journey. This did not surprise me since they had been in an enclosure all their lives and it had always meant food and safety.

So now you see why we need to use anthropomorphism constructively. We must have some reason to believe that there is potential for analogous experiences, and we must have a good understanding of the animal's ecological, evolutionary, and individual history. Then we are free to use our empathy to make some prediction, which we must then evaluate. If it holds up, we are in a good position to make increasingly better predictions, and perhaps then we can begin to claim some understanding of what it's like to be someone or something else.

Recently, many of the very concepts that so entranced Darwin, such as animal emotion and cognitive ability, have returned to scientific prominence, as I will outline below. This has been partly due to dissatisfaction with the limitations imposed by strict adherence to Morgan's Canon. But we have not simply come full circle back to 1872. Scientists have not returned to discussing anger, jealousy, nobility, and joy in all manner of insects, birds, and mammals. As Marian Dawkins (1980:11) points out:

> Present day studies on the mental experiences of animals are far more rigorous and experimental than they were in the nineteenth century. The lessons of Behaviourism have not been lost. Perhaps the study of mental events in animals has advanced precisely because it has had to stand up to Behaviourists and justify itself in the face of their criticisms.

51

Let me briefly outline a few areas where an anthropomorphic perspective has been helpful.

## Animal Learning

Some of the most interesting studies in animal learning are those that question some of the basic assumptions of the Behaviorist tradition. One of the most significant sets of findings in recent years has been that many species seem particularly disposed to learn certain things that have special adaptive significance in their everyday lives. The most dramatic demonstration of this has been the Garcia Effect, in which rats rapidly learn the taste or odor associated with the one-time presentation of a food linked to an illness often following the food by as many as twelve hours. Garcia approached the issue in a very straightforward way, reasoning that if he were an animal that ate garbage and was incapable of vomiting, he'd surely want to know what made him sick. As he explained (Garcia 1981:151):

> I always use anthropomorphism and teleology to predict animal behavior because this works better than most learning theories. I could rationalize this heresy by pointing to our common neurosensory systems or to convergent evolutionary forces. But, in truth, I merely put myself in the animal's place.

## Animal Communication

As with animal learning, most studies of just a few years ago focused on the objective description of animal sounds and postures and their contexts. These signals were largely seen as behaviors that were motivated by some basic biological need and responded to in some reflexive way. Recently there has been considerable interest in analyzing animal communication in terms of the message that the animal *intends* to send and the behavior that it *intends* to elicit in the recipient. There has also been renewed interest in the extensive parallels across species of certain common signals that are conveyed in common ways. Of particular interest are studies of gestures and facial expressions in nonhuman as well as human primates, which tend to vindicate many of Darwin's writings on animal expression.

## Comparative Psychopathology

The entire approach to using animals to model human mental disorders was questioned for years because of the assumption that there was no animal mind, and thus there can be no madness without mentality. It is this resistance to the basic premise of mental disorders in animals that, I feel, forced H. F. Harlow to go to such extremes of maternal deprivation to produce monkeys that were so clearly disturbed (Harlow and Mears 1979). Today there is continued use of animal models, but with far greater emphasis on the alleviation of disorders than on the induction of them. Still, there are many researchers who make use of such methods yet would be unwilling to admit that the animals they are using as models of depressed humans are themselves "feeling depressed." Even Harlow recognized that the problem with comparative psychopathology was not its reliance on anthropomorphism per se, but on the extent to which humans share the experiences the animals endure. He wrote (Harlow and Mears 1979:218), "Perhaps our greatest, most significant discovery is that human behavior generalizes to monkeys, whether or not monkey behavior generalizes to humans."

## The Human/Companion-Animal Bond

Scientists have traditionally sought to avoid anthropomorphism, and since we are most likely to be anthropomorphic about the animals we know best, scientists have tended to shun the study of the behavior of pets and livestock, and particularly man's interaction with them. The opening of this vital new field was delayed for years. Scientists rejected farmers and pet owners as a source of valid ethological hypotheses, and as a result they have both ignored a vast resource and alienated some of the most able observers from the aims and methods of science. Fortunately this trend has been reversing (see Beck and Katcher 1983), and I look forward to the time, not far off, when we can recruit pet owners into the ranks of objective contributors to our understanding of animal behavior.

## Applied Ethology

Another discipline that has benefited from the scientific application of anthropomorphic ideas is applied animal behavior. This field seeks to use principles of ethology and comparative psychology to modify animal behavior or adjust environments to produce desirable behaviors. A few years ago the notion that animals in captivity might suffer boredom, stress, loneliness, or similar conditions would have been considered mere sentimentalism by "hard" scientists. However, a growing number of people found such ideas useful for generating hypotheses about how to improve captive environments. You can see a nice example of this at the National Zoo in Washington, D.C. Starting with the assumption that apes can be bored and depressed, National Zoo staff have provided the apes with a variety of unusual edible foods and assorted playthings to maintain their interest. The effects of this on behavior can be measured, and the hypothesis evaluated.

A similar empathic perspective has helped the study of misbehavior in companion animals. Borchelt (1983) has found it useful to regard many of the destructive behaviors shown by pet dogs left alone to be the consequence of "separation anxiety." By attending to the cues that would exaggerate or reduce this hypothetical state, he has been able to design effective treatment programs.

## Animal Welfare

As indicated earlier, it would have been unthinkable not so long ago to propose scientific studies of animal suffering. Now there is great concern over assessing animals' experience of pain and the response of animals to different conditions of care. This change has not simply been the result of increased sensitivity to the lobbying efforts of the animal-welfare and animal-rights movements; rather, it is a true reflection of many scientists' realization that these questions, rooted in anthropomorphic projections, are timely, interesting, biologically valid, and morally significant.

## Conclusion

In summary, I hope I have clarified the difference among various forms of anthropomorphism and have convinced you of its slowly growing respectability as a scientific tool. There will always be barriers to trying to understand other species, just as there are barriers to understanding other human beings. But it is a disservice to ourselves and to our fellow human and nonhuman creatures to regard any attempt to comprehend their experiences and feelings as merely irrational or sentimental.

## Select Bibliography

Beck, A.M., and A.H. Katcher. 1983. *Between pets and people: The importance of animal companionship.* New York: G.P. Putnam's Sons.

Borchelt, P. 1983. Separation-elicited behavior problems in dogs. In *New perspectives on our lives with companion animals,* ed. A.H. Katcher and A.M. Beck. Philadelphia: University of Pennsylvania Press.

Breland, K., and M. Breland. 1966. *Animal behavior.* Toronto: Macmillan.

Broadhurst, P.L. 1963. *The science of animal behaviour.* Baltimore: Penguin.

Dawkins, M.S. 1980. *Animal suffering: The science of animal welfare.* New York: Chapman and Hall.

Darwin, C. 1872. *The expression of the emotions in man and animals.* Reprinted 1965. Chicago: University of Chicago Press.

Garcia, J. 1981. Tilting at the paper mills of academe. *American Psychologist* 36(2):149–58.

Harlow, H.F., and C. Mears. 1979. *The human model: Primate perspectives.* New York: John Wiley and Sons.

Lorenz, K.Z. 1952. *King Solomon's ring.* London: Methuen.

Morgan, C.L. 1894. *Introduction to comparative psychology.* London: Walter Scott.

Pavlov, I.P. 1960. *Conditioned reflexes.* New York: Dover.

Tinbergen, N. 1953. *The herring gull's world.* London: Collins.

Washburn, M.F. 1917. *The animal mind.* New York: Macmillan.

Watson, J.B. 1924. *Psychology from the standpoint of a behaviorist.* Philadelphia: Lippincott.

# Neoteny in American
# Perceptions of Animals

## Elizabeth A. Lawrence

In American culture there is a strong tendency to anthropomorphize certain animals, and more specifically, to view animals as juveniles. While neoteny, which refers to the retention of youthful traits into adulthood, is a human biological characteristic, it is also a psychological as well as a physical condition, real or not, that humans often perceive in species other than their own. This chapter discusses the role of neoteny in American perceptions of animals, including both our animal associates from the real world and creatures from the realm of human imagination.

# Anthropomorphized Animals in Amusement Parks

Consider, for example, the popularity of the fanciful animal characters inhabiting Walt Disney's Magic Kingdoms. The huge numbers of enthusiastic visitors who enter these celebrated amusement parks represent a remarkable and revealing contemporary phenomenon. Certainly a strong need is being met through experiences in these parks, and it is safe to say that a significant share of their appeal derives from the characters which, in various forms, are encountered there. One of the highlights of the Disney park experience is the storybook and comic-strip figures that come alive to enable patrons to mingle with and even talk to and touch them. At the Magic Kingdoms, adults and children have the opportunity to interact with a mischievous duck named Donald, very much humanized, although not to the degree of what must surely be the most highly anthropomorphized of all fanciful animal characters, Mickey Mouse (Figure 1), official host at Disney's kingdoms. One of the earliest cartoon stars, and undeniably the most famous, Mickey is still referred to by Americans as "everybody's friend," a "cute little rascal," and a "nice little person." Virtually no one perceives this familar creature as a mouse! Characters like Mickey, the March Hare, Pluto, and Goofy appear larger than life. Ironically, although they appear adult in stature, they are consistently juvenile in both form and behavior.

In addition to the domestic sphere populated by creatures such as ducks, dogs, and tame mice, the realm of wild nature is also vividly represented in the Magic Kingdoms. One sails through the jaws of a whale to discover Geppetto's village, or embarks on an undersea journey of exploration with Captain Nemo in a submarine. On the most exotic of all rides, the Jungle Cruise, the traveler passes through many simulated dangerous experiences involving elephants, rhinos, alligators, and head hunters—always, of course, ending with a safe return to "civilization" (where, as a guide points out, much greater risks await on nearby expressways).

According to anthropologist and African specialist Colin Turnbull (1981:26), countless American tourists are disappointed by their actual African safaris, and speak of being more successful at finding the partici-

*Figure 1. Mickey Mouse and Donald Duck, two of the highly anthropomorphized animal characters created by The Walt Disney Co. Both characters are internationally recognized and both exhibit juvenile behavioral and physical traits. (Illustrations provided by The Walt Disney Co.)*

pation in nature they seek by visiting a Disney park. In trying to explain why experiences at a Disney park can seem more "real" and "natural" than those in Africa, Turnbull concludes that too much separation between man and nature is perceived by the average tourist on safari. The game parks that now permit only secure, structured access to wildlife, he believes, can no longer provide the sense of oneness with and participation in the natural world that is sought. Consequently, today's traveler merely passes through the African terrain, and does not feel it, smell it, or experience it authentically. Turnbull (1981:33–34) concludes that a Disney park seems to answer the longing for a lost sense of contact with animals in a way that makes it both possible and respectable, and which through fantasy renders the gap between the human and natural worlds less formidable or, at least for a time, nonexistent.

But beyond this, I believe it is in large measure the juvenilization of the fanciful characters in the Magic Kingdoms which gives them their special capacity of seeming to bridge the gap that separates man and animal in the modern industrial world. From the dressed-up clownish bears who hug excited youngsters to the submerged plastic hippos whose huge eyes blink at passengers from murky jungle waters, visitors are led to relate to them not as mature equals, but as children.

One does not have to travel to a Disney park, of course, to see that in contemporary American society it is common practice to anthropomorphize and in particular to neotenize—both physically and behaviorally—many animals that are part of daily life. Creatures like the familiar and beloved Snoopy, Charlie Brown's dog, are consistently depicted as immature—not just as they appear in the comics, but in decorative design, toys, games, and television programs. Humanized and immensely appealing, it is the beagle's juvenile form and character that make people relate to him. Yet paradoxically, it may be only because he is a dog, and thus separated from our species, that we empathize and identify with him.

# Neoteny and Its Influence on Perceptions of Animals

Neoteny is a condition in which youthful characteristics are retained in the adult form of an animal. Human beings are considered a neotenous species (Figure 2) because they retain into maturity certain traits that were once exclusively juvenile features of our closest primate relatives. Adult chimpanzees, for example, lose the flat face they exhibit in the juvenile stage and develop a protruding muzzle and receding forehead. Man's flat face, high-domed skull, reduced pelt, upright frame, small teeth, and large eyes are all features of infant and young apes that are lost in adulthood. Thus man, as compared to other primates, has become neotenized (Desmond 1979:160). Juvenilization is behavioral as well as physical, for the prolonged childhood of mankind includes social as well as biological traits. Weston La Barre (1954) points out that increasing social dependency is directly related to the "infantilization" of human physical traits.

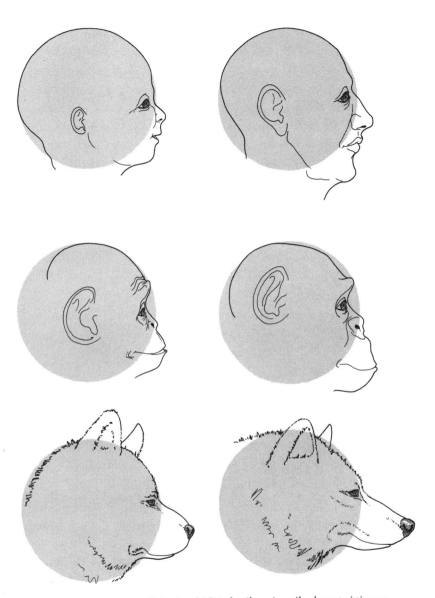

*Figure 2. Neoteny is a condition in which infantile or juvenile characteristics are preserved in the adult condition. Pictured are the heads of both infant and adult humans, chimpanzees, and wolves. The heads are drawn not to scale but to show relative proportions. Compared to the chimp and the wolf, the adult human head is more domed and the face less projecting—traits that show that humans have become more neotenized than other animals. (Illustration by Sally Bensusen.)*

Related to the human progression toward juvenilization is the fact that in the process of domesticating the familiar animals there has been a general tendency to bring selective pressures on them which often resulted in neotenization. Charles Darwin noted that the process of domestication operated through artificial selection by man in a way analogous to the evolution of species taking place by means of natural selection. He drew attention to the importance of changes in animals brought on by domestication in *On the Origin of Species* (1859), and in his two-volume work, *The Variation of Animals and Plants Under Domestication* (1868). Darwin (1868 1:92–95) observed some differences between wild and domestic forms consistently found in various species. For example, the Yorkshire breed of pig demonstrates the shortening and broadening of the head typical of domesticates. Most domesticated species, with the exception of horses and cats, show similar head changes (Clutton-Brock 1981:24).

Consciously or unconsciously, in order to satisfy human needs and tastes, mankind has selectively neotenized real animals as well as cartoon characters. Shedding light on this process, ethologist Konrad Lorenz (1981:164–65) has described the innate releasing "schema" for human parental-care responses. He proposes that the physical configuration of a high and slightly bulging forehead, large brain case in proportion to the face, big eyes, rounded cheeks, and short, stubby limbs calls forth an adult nurturing response to such a "lovable" object, eliciting feelings of tenderness. The same positive reactions are elicited by animals who exhibit these juvenile traits. This phenomenon, of course, is well known to doll and toy manufacturers, who rely on such an "infant schema" in creating forms with the exaggerated attributes of small children, such has big head in proportion to body and huge eyes, which increase the protective-releasing effect of "cute" dolls and stuffed animals. Entertainment producers and cartoonists make full use of it as well. Biologist Stephen Jay Gould (1980:95–107) has shown how Disney artists over the years have progressively neotenized the form of Mickey Mouse, so that his development mirrors the trend toward youthful features characteristic of human evolution.

Neotenization is particularly evident in man's close companion ani-

*Figure 3. The chihuahua, with its large domed head, large eyes, small body, and small limbs, has been bred by humans as a neotenized form that often serves as a child surrogate. (Illustration by Sally Bensusen.)*

mal, the dog. Though some breeds still bear an outward resemblance to the ancestral wolf, many others have been dramatically modified for human purposes. Striking examples of "man-made" types of dogs are Pekingeses and Boston terriers. Such canines exhibit features of the infant schema, and often in adult form approximate the body size of a human newborn. Drastic alterations have caused many dog breeds to retain to maturity certain characteristics of juvenile or even fetal wolves, such as short facial region of the skull, large brain case, big eyes, short legs, curly tail, and soft fur (Clutton-Brock 1981:39). In chihuahuas (Figure 3), diminutive size, prominent eyes, and a domed skull with retention of an open fontanelle serve to juvenilize it. And chihuahuas, as many veterinarians discover, often function as child surrogates.

Neotenization of familiar animals is not confined to morphology. All common domesticated mammals have undergone changes that appear to be the result of retention of the juvenile, submissive behavior of the young animal to its parent. This is of great advantage to the human owner who wishes to maintain dominance over the animal. Undoubtedly this trait has been highly selected for by inbreeding, and is correlated with the neotenization of anatomical features (Clutton-Brock 1981:25).

## Neotenizing: Roots in Childhood

In our society, learning to anthropomorphize animals and to perceive them as juveniles generally begins in infancy. Neotenized stuffed animals are the earliest crib companions. Babies' first picture books and nursery rhyme collections communicate images like "The Three Little Kittens"—naughty children who disobey their mother and must be chastised. Large-headed, wide-eyed felines dressed in snowsuits vividly convey the message of foolish youth in need of adult control (e.g., illustration, Szekeres 1983:22).

I have observed that wild species of animals—those that remain outside the familiar human domain—are perceived and portrayed without neotenous distortions. Such relative realism is used to differentiate the wild from the tame. The Big Bad Wolf in "The Three Little Pigs," for example, is anthropomorphized as an evil villain (see illustration, Szekeres 1983:12). As an antagonist to the domestic realm, he is cast as outsider and destroyer, portrayed as aggressive and sinister. To indicate these qualities, such animals are given features opposite from those of neoteny: low foreheads, long snouts (see the adult wolf head in Figure 2), and small, narrow eyes which widen only momentarily in a gesture of satisfaction from some malicious act. The audience is appropriately repelled.

Recently a new hero, this time from outer space, became one of the most appealing characters of our time. A look at "E.T.," the Extra-Terrestrial (star of a movie of the early 1980s), shows him to be extremely neotenized both in appearance and behavior. He has an extraordinarily large head and huge eyes in proportion to his body, and acts the part of a child (see also discussions in Beck and Katcher, 1983:190). When he must hide among toy animals and dolls he is well camouflaged, for he is made in their image. Many messages are conveyed by E.T.'s visit to our troubled planet; one of the clearest is that only children can discover and understand his true significance. To remedy the many ills and crises of our world, then, it is necessary first to become childlike and make a fresh start. Hardly a new message, this is a timely and popularized version of traditional ones: "Whosoever shall not receive the kingdom of God as a little child, he shall in no wise enter therein" (Mark 10:15), and "A little child shall lead them" (Isaiah 11:6).

# Prehistoric Peoples' Perceptions of Animals

To understand the perceptions of animals that predominate in contemporary industrialized society, one must go back in human history approximately ten thousand years, and consider the transformations wrought during the Neolithic Revolution. It is impossible to overestimate the importance of mankind's shift from hunter–gatherer to domesticator of plants and animals during that era. The consequent sedentarization of many human groups led to profound alterations in social structure, culture, and mode of existence, and ultimately to urban living. Rooted in some of these changes and in the ethos of human domination over nature that arose in the Western world, is mankind's relentless war on the environment, our never-ending quest to exert control.

As is often pointed out, mankind has followed the dictates of a hunting way of life for fully 99 percent of our existence on earth. Hunting peoples of necessity had, and may still have, intimate relationships with animals and a keen understanding of the nature and behavior of prey species in order to ensure hunting success. It is known from studies of art and other archaeological evidence, as well as from ethnographic analogy using data from contemporary hunters, that such an existence in many cases is correlated with underlying respect for animals. I am not discussing here the issue of cruelty versus kindness. Many hunters express hostility toward their prey and may treat them (and their domesticated animals as well) with what our society would call brutality, or at the very least with extreme exploitativeness and lack of sympathy (e.g., Turnbull 1961:101, 252); but the animals in these cases are not generally, so far as we know, anthropomorphized or neotenized. Their adult status does not seem to be called into question. Indeed, certain highly regarded animal species often are imitated by hunters who hope to become enough like them to know them at every level of being. Early people, like those in some of the world's remaining nonindustrialized societies today, no doubt longed to acquire certain powers and abilities of animals which they recognized as superior to their own. Through rites and ceremonies, mystical union leading to the sharing of a vital universal force was sought.

For early societies, human life in every dimension was controlled by the ebb and flow of animal life. Man's dominance over other creatures lay far in the future. Cro-Magnon cave art portrays beasts in the splendor and might of full maturity, possessing vibrant and realistically proportioned forms. With the development of man's drive for manipulation and mastery of the natural world, and the rise of anthropocentric ideology of domination to support it, perceptions of human–animal interaction were altered irrevocably. The culmination of this change from human beings seeking to acquire the power of other animals to perceiving that relationship "the other way around" is, as Turnbull (1981:31) points out, clearly expressed in "our folk tales of today" which "tell of animals acquiring human powers such as speech and abstract thought." By casting them in the mold of juvenile pupils to be instructed, the animals in our lives—both actual and in fantasy—come more surely under our influence, and are bent to our desires.

# Non-Western Perceptions of Animals

In order to shed light on American perceptions of animals as they have been influenced by our Western intellectual heritage, let us look briefly at some evidence available from non-Western societies. By considering the views of such diverse peoples as Plains Indians, the Naskapi hunters of Labrador, Australian Aborigines, and pastoralists like the Nuer of Africa's Upper Nile, one can highlight certain contrasts which serve to make our own outlook more intelligible.

## Plains Indians

Central to the traditional ethos of native peoples in the Great Plains is the concept that animals have something of significance to communicate to people. Animals impart essential practical information and guidance as well as wisdom and spiritual insight. Far from being dependent children or incomplete adults, animals may be respected teachers with valuable repositories of knowledge. The famed Sioux leader Sitting Bull, for example, was saved from death by the warnings of a meadowlark, and from then on he often communicated with members of that species whom he considered relatives (Vestal 1932:22). Plenty-Coups, most respected chief of the Crow tribe, received valuable aid and information from his special helper the chickadee, the one "least in strength but strongest of mind among birds" (Linderman 1930).

The earth for a Plains native is shared with other animals as equals and brothers. The universe is conceptualized as a circle, with all forms of life on the same plane, each having a different but equally important role to play. This worldview is the opposite of our linear, hierarchical scheme in which each form of life is ranked according to its purported complexity or value. Described by Aristotle as the *scala natura*, later known as the ladder of life or Great Chain of Being (Lovejoy 1936), this mode of perceiving nature is an integral part of Western ideology.

Granted total participation in the circle of life by Plains Indians, animals in their scheme are not seen as juveniles. In fact, animals in native American creation stories often possess both the wisdom and the power to help in making the earth and even in bringing mankind into existence (Marriott and Rachlin 1968:38–43)—surely no task for the immature or unwise. Thus perceptions of animal ability and participation contrast sharply with those recorded in the Judeo-Christian Genesis version of the Earth's and man's beginning in which God creates everything and mandates expected behavior for all creatures, with animals subservient to man and man subservient to God.

## The Naskapi

Among many groups of traditional hunting peoples, particularly those of northern latitudes exemplified by tribes like the Naskapi, respect and admiration for prey animals and strict mutual obligations between hunter and hunted assure that man will continue to be bountifully supplied with food and other necessities. Slain animals must always be the object of proscribed rituals to ensure that their spirits will be appeased and their fellow creatures in the future will allow themselves to be killed for human sustenance. Animal guardians or masters of each prey species release game only if hunters afford proper treatment of remains and cause no waste. "Hunting is a holy occupation" (Speck 1937). Differing drastically from our view of man as master of living "resources" which have been placed on earth expressly for human use, the Naskapi belief system preserves balance between people and nature as manifestations of one and the same power.

## The Australian Aborigines

Australian Aborigines have a remarkable relationship with nature in which there is perceptual continuity between human beings and animal, plant, or object forms. "The Australian does not draw the same distinction between man and nature that Europeans do; the consistent elements of nature are parts of the tribe, as the members of the tribe are parts of nature" (Giddens 1979:95). Aboriginal tribes exhibit totemic social structure, the intricacy and complexity of which have made totems of central importance to the understanding of the sociology of religion (Durkheim 1915). Totemism, symbolizing the close alliance between humans and nature, is a cognitive scheme used to express and codify a person's place within the universe. Totems, which are often animals from the immediate environment like the kangaroo and emu, define and delineate social relationships by positing a mystical union with that animal through common descent. The essential concept is that of oneness between all members of the totem species and the people of a clan, who often seek to honor and emulate the species (Spencer and Gillen 1899:112–27). As expressed by Roheim (1925:36), "at the root of totemism" is the "psychical survival of a biological unity with environment." Absent is any idea of a status for nature of less than full maturity. (Interestingly, dingoes are believed by some scientists to have accompanied the Aboriginal peoples into what is now Australia when they migrated there many thousands of years ago. Yet from all evidence these canines have never been neotenized.)

## The Nuer

Pastoralists are members of societies that derive a substantial share of their livelihood from grazing stock. Examples can still be drawn from various areas of the world where people live in a state of intimacy and interdependence with animals such as sheep, horses, camels, yaks, and llamas and fill a large portion of their needs through products from their herds. Often these societies exhibit interactions with animals so close as to be symbiotic. Tribes comprising the African cattle complex, in particular, have been the object of a great deal of study by social scientists, and represent a remarkable phenomenon in which bovine animals are inextricably woven into the socio-cultural fabric of everyday life.

The cattle-herding Nuer, for example, live mainly on milk, generally partaking of meat only when a cow dies or is sacrificed in a religious ceremony. In return for what they provide, the animals are cared for and nurtured assiduously by herdsmen who live only for the welfare of their beasts (Figure 4). Thus cattle and men sustain life by their reciprocal services; men and beasts form a single community of the closest kind with "solidarity of interests." Cattle herds are not mere necessities of life, but the central and highly esteemed elements around which existence revolves. They represent status, ethnic and personal identity, wealth, social relationships, religion, and artistic expression—in short, all that is good and desirable—to these people with "the herdsman's outlook on the world" (Evans-Pritchard 1940). Identified with as brethren, admired as friends, cattle are scarcely viewed as juvenile by the Nuer. Rather, the animals are equals, relatives—sometimes even demigods—full participants in the dynamic cycle of a life in harmony with nature.

# Perceptions of Animals in Western Thought

In contrast to these societies, our culture generally endorses not a continuity between mankind and nature, but a vast gulf. At the root of this long-standing schism are many complex factors which include our intellectual legacy from René Descartes, the seventeenth-century mathematician and

*Figure 4. Humped Zebu cattle play a pivotal role in many of the "cattle" cultures of Africa, including that of the Nuer.*

philosopher whose ideas "changed the course of Western thought" (Wilson 1969:vii–xxxii). Cartesianism is a cognitive scheme embracing sharp dichotomies such as observer/observed, body/mind, and human/animal, so firmly entrenched in Western perceptions that their absolute existence is regarded by many people as "objective truth." In the dualistic organization of Cartesianism, animals are viewed as beings of another order from people, machines without awareness, sentience, or possession of immortal souls (Descartes 1637). It is easy to see that this system of thought makes not only logical, but imperative, the idea of man as master over nature. And, I suggest, it is a short leap indeed from perceiving nonhuman life forms as different, separate, and inferior to perceiving them as juvenile.

Among the explanations for why we in Western culture, and particularly in contemporary American society, neotenize our animals as we do is our need to *gain a sense of control* over them. As docile and playful "children," they may be relegated to a separate category, without full citizenship in our world.

In popularizing an image of big-headed, pop-eyed, green-vested, fat-bellied frogs frittering away their time, for example, the obvious message is that we do not take the species seriously. It may follow that we can more easily continue to drain their swamp habitats without compunction, for we have no sense of responsibility toward their domain as we do toward our own. On the other hand, the likeness of a tree frog painted by a contemporary Australian Aboriginal artist (author's collection) clearly focuses on what I call "frogness." The central concern of the depiction is to illustrate the ways this particular animal obtained the capacities unique to its being.

In stories typified by "The Three Bears," we continue to lead children to conceptualize certain animals as cute and cuddly, even as they assume an air of grouchiness (see Szekeres 1983:26–31). Bears in this archetypal tale are often portrayed as bumbling idiots, easily taken advantage of by opportunists like Goldilocks. Juvenilized creatures offer people no competition, and relieve us of the responsibility to understand and respect them for qualities intrinsic to their species. Light is shed on this phenomenon by a recent cartoon featuring a serious and adult-proportioned father bear phoning the insurance company to make sure his policy covers missing porridge and mussed beds. Humor in this case arises from the sophisticated response of the bear. Ironically, the child-like petulance of whining about loss of food and intrusion has been replaced by a cool, calculated adult response to theft and trespass. We find this funny precisely because, according to our way of viewing the world, it is not going to happen.

By anthropomorphizing and especially by neotenizing selected species of animals, we are able to impute moral qualities to them in differing measure and to suit our own purposes. Through these mechanisms species can be assigned varying rank and status according to their usefulness or lack of it in the human scheme. As Benson (1983:82) points out, when viewing the animal as child, if "the value of an animal consists in its docility, playfulness, and charm as a human companion," then "animals that fail to meet such standards may be written off as of no account."

There is ambivalence in the way most people in our society view the wild. We admire it for its beauty and freedom, yet at the same time we fear it and strive to conquer it. An ongoing battle of wild-versus-tame is part of the American heritage (Lawrence 1982), and animal figures from tales and fantasies influence and express our perceptions of a species' role and value. Thus predators like the wolf in "The Three Little Pigs" come to be viewed as evil incarnate, threatening both man and the realm of neotenized domesticates that we control, as represented by pigs.

The wolf in "Little Red Riding Hood" is a highly symbolic figure as well. During anthropological field work in the Great Plains states, I interviewed a number of wildlife refuge personnel who felt under constant pressure from regional stockmen to eliminate wolves from the range. Terming the phenomenon the "Little Red Riding Hood Syndrome," these officials indicated its considerable prevalence and influence on the sentiment which causes people to favor prey and abhor predator species. Often, they said, pressures come from people who want to hunt the prey species themselves and feel the wolves represent competition (Lawrence 1982:244–62).

In a similar way, the "Bambi Complex" refers to use of a highly neotenized deer as symbolic of innocence and mildness, a creature which, though belonging to the wild realm, will occasionally flee to man's domain for protection (Lawrence 1982:254–55). With a huge head dwarfing its trunk and a pair of oversized eyes with pupils and lashes (Shaw 1941), Disney's Bambi arouses sympathy and nurturance and a sense of parenthood toward this relatively sociable species that sometimes responds to human attention.

Confused by the paradox of the wild and the tame, in our society we are additionally afflicted with a deep-rooted ambivalence concerning the exploitation of domesticated animals for food. Many Americans, in fact, live with a kind of psychic denial that the flesh they eat is really part of an animal. In the past, when the majority of people in the United States were rural, the slaughter of animals was close at hand and had to be accepted. Universally, hunters and pastoralists have been able to reconcile admiration and even reverence for an animal species with consumption of it, and have ingrained cultural patterns for so doing. But for many of us today this constitutes an insoluble dilemma. One way of coping with such a quandary in contemporary American society is our paternalistic response of

72

neotenizing the farm animals we raise to eat so they do not have to be dealt with as equals.

We teach our children from infancy to imagine blissful barnyard friends who eat grass all day in the sunshine and go to warm snug stalls at night. Farmer Brown of children's books is not a farm operator using intensive methods, but a caring steward. He provides not only life's necessities to his dependent and allegedly happy charges, but even leisure, affection, and an opportunity for socialization with their fellows. Meat animals, especially pigs, are sometimes depicted as jolly folks, indulging in hedonistic activities and glamorous escapades like those of Miss Piggy. It is significant that even in our modern world few parents fail to recite "This Little Piggy Went to Market," with appropriate gestures, to delighted offspring. Tacit duplicity assures all but the most ruthlessly honest that the pig is going on a trip for groceries, not making its final trip to the slaughterhouse.

# The Possible Influence of the Fear of Death

We in present-day America have been called a death-denying society, for many people observed in daily life and actions seem to reject the idea of their own mortality. Certainly we are a youth-oriented culture. It is probable that by neotenizing our closest animal associates, who then never seem to grow old, we identify with the carefree merry-making that characterizes our fairy-tale view of them. By this means they serve to rejuvenate us as well as protect us from the reality of the old age and death we dread. Perhaps, in these troubled times, it is really human extinction we fear, with a consequent take-over of the world by less destructive animals. If so, our juvenilization of them reassures us they will fail and reinforces our status as their masters. If our species is believed to be the goal of evolution, the others can be seen merely as poor imitations trying to emulate us.

Mickey Mouse, our dearest friend from fantasy, is more than sixty years old, yet retains his prepubescent voice and childlike ways. Through his eyes we see the world afresh. Miraculously, he does not remain unchanged but rather becomes younger, and so he truly defies death through the process of neoteny. In current usage, something that is "Mickey

Mouse" is not quite adequate or up to standard—trivial, foolish, or a bit of a sham, perhaps. (A "Mick" in college still designates an easy course.) Helping to sum up Mickey's place in our society, this linguistic usage is indicative of his neoteny, something is indeed lacking—maturity. Expressing the idea that growing old gives wholeness to life, a sense of completion that youth alone cannot provide, Robert Browning (1941:860) has wisely called our later years "the last of life, for which the first was made." Because neoteny has kept him an eternal child, Mickey can express certain things about our world that lack the perspective of an experienced adult.

# Conclusion

Mickey Mouse is also a reminder of our unfulfilled desire for unity with the animal world, which we project through fantasy, and of the gap between man and nature that has been created by our sense of superiority over nonhuman forms of life. Mickey personifies the strange modern notion that animals should take on human traits rather than that we should respect animals for their own capacities. Because his animality is camouflaged, Mickey also represents that uncertainty which we as human beings feel toward exploited species of animals. Mickey's ambiguous and comic figure is somehow able to stand squarely in his yellow outsized shoes between us and the guilt we may feel at our mistreatment of animals. For we celebrate the innocence and charm of friendly and appealing mice in literature and fantasy even as we almost unquestioningly exploit (and exterminate) millions of the same species for the benefit of our own kind.

Simpler to relate to than a human child, the irrepressible child–mouse character delights us, no doubt making it easier to overlook the animal qualities we see and perhaps fear in ourselves. Our affectionate reaction to Mickey's wide-set eyes and broad smile and our cheering on of his madcap antics are universal testimonials of appreciation for his youth. The popularity of neotenized figures like Mickey is undoubtedly related to American affluence, materialistic values, and alienation from kin, all factors which make us prone to indulge in the "pampered pet" syndrome.

As a dressed-up character, dear, familiar, and childlike, yet a member of a species that is generally held in low esteem, this paradoxical mouse might cause us to reflect on our responsibility to the natural world and to question the wisdom of neoteny in our perception of animals. He reminds us that it is our species which must now determine the balance between the wild and the tame in a world so rapidly becoming the domain of the tame at the expense of the wild.

Although Mickey tells us very little about mice, he tells us a great deal about ourselves.

# Selective Bibliography

Beck, A.M. and A.H. Katcher 1983. *Between pets and people: The importance of animal companionship.* New York: G.P. Putnam's Sons.

Benson, T.L. 1983. The clouded mirror. In *Ethics and animals,* ed. H.B. Miller and W.H. Williams, pp. 79–90. Clifton, New Jersey: Humana.

Browning, R. 1941. Rabbi Ben Ezra. In *Great poems of the English language,* compiler W.A. Briggs, p. 860. New York: Tudor.

Clutton-Brock, J. 1981. *Domesticated animals from early times.* Austin: University of Texas Press.

Darwin, C. 1859. *On the origin of species.* Reprinted 1967, pp. 212–16, 466–69. New York: Athenaeum.

————. 1868. *The variation of animals and plants under domestication,* 2 vols. New York: Orange Judd & Co.

Descartes, R. 1637. *Discourse on method and the Meditations.* Reprinted 1979. New York: Penguin.

Desmond, A.J. 1979. *The ape's reflexion.* New York: Dial.

Durkheim, E. 1915. *The elementary forms of the religious life,* trans. J.W. Swain. Reprinted 1965. New York: Free Press.

Evans-Pritchard, E.E. 1940. *The Nuer.* Reprinted 1974, pp. 16–50. New York: Oxford University Press.

Finch, C. 1983. *The art of Walt Disney.* New York: Abrams.

Giddens, A. 1978. *Emile Durkheim.* New York: Penguin.

Gould, S.J. 1980. *The panda's thumb.* New York: W.W. Norton.

*Holy Bible* 1929. Standard American Edition of the Revised Version. New York: Nelson.

La Barre, W. 1954. *The human animal.* Reprinted 1972, pp. 156, 304. Chicago: University of Chicago Press.

Lawrence, E.A. 1986. In the Mick of time: Reflections on Disney's ageless mouse. *Journal of Popular Culture* 20:65–72.

———. 1982. *Rodeo: An anthropologist looks at the wild and the tame.* Knoxville: University of Tennessee Press.

Linderman, F.B. 1930. *Plenty-Coups: Chief of the Crows.* Reprinted 1972, p. 66. New York: Day.

Lorenz, K. 1981. *The foundations of ethology.* New York: Simon & Schuster.

Lovejoy, A.O. 1936. *The great chain of being.* Reprinted 1973. Cambridge: Harvard University Press.

Marriott, A., and C.K. Rachlin 1968. *American Indian mythology.* New York: New American Library.

Roheim, G. 1925. *Australian totemism.* London: Allen & Unwin.

Shaw, M., adapted by. 1941. *Walt Disney's Bambi.* Reprinted 1982. Racine, Wisconsin: Golden Books.

Speck, F.G. 1935. *Naskapi.* Reprinted 1977, pp. 72–127. Norman: University of Oklahoma Press.

Spencer, B., and F.J. Gillen 1899. *The native tribes of central Australia.* New York: Macmillan.

Szekeres, C., illustrated by. 1983. *A child's first book of nursery tales.* Racine, Wisconsin: Golden Books.

Turnbull, C. 1961. *The forest people.* New York: Simon & Schuster.

———. 1981. East African safari. *Natural History,* 5:26, 29–34.

Vestal, S. 1932. *Sitting Bull: Champion of the Sioux.* Cambridge, Mass.: Houghton Mifflin.

Wilson, M.D., ed. 1969. *The essential Descartes.* New York: New American Library.

# The Wolf:
# Fact and Fiction

**Erich Klinghammer**

One day at dusk in 1962, at the edge of the Winnebago Indian Reservation in Nebraska, I saw my first wild wolves. A friend and I were coming around a hill on horseback when we came upon two wolves, no more than two hundred feet away and looking straight at us. Seconds later they vanished silently into a ravine. We galloped to the top of the hill hoping to see them again, but they were gone.

That initial impression never left me, and has exerted a powerful influence over the rest of my life. It led me to a career in ethology where the wolf has been a major focus of my scientific work. Over the years my colleagues and I have learned much about wolves. However, if we want to understand wolves in the context of the theme of "Perceptions of Animals in American Culture," we need to go back into history to understand where we are today.

# The Wolf in Historical Perspective

The most comprehensive review of this topic is found in *Of Wolves and Men* by Barry Lopez (1978). Long before the age of scientific inquiry, each culture had its own perception of the wolf. What little factual information that existed was usually embellished, exaggerated, distorted, or twisted to fit an image based not on careful observation but on imagination, myth, and anthropomorphic projections of human characteristics onto the wolf.

According to Lopez, the medieval European mind was obsessed with images of wolves, and the belief in werewolves was widespread. In those days wolves were equated with thieves, and to call for "the wolf's head" meant a sentence of death to a man accused of wrongdoing. He could then be killed by anyone without fear of legal reprisal. In Dante's *Divina Commedia*, the wolf appears as a symbol of greed and fraud. Toward the end of the *Commedia*, Dante refers to seducers, hypocrites, magicians, thieves, and liars as those possessing "the sins of the wolf." Medieval peasants also called famine "the wolf," and avaricious landlords were called "wolves" (Lopez 1978).

The wolf in old European fables is not willfully evil; the wolf's wicked nature is ascribed to its having been born a wolf. In fairy tales, however, the wolf is usually represented as malicious, capable of great evil, and only occasionally as warm and devoted. In Lopez's discussion of "Red Riding Hood," we are treated to some psychoanalytical interpretations in which the wolf is seen as seducer of the red-hooded girl, an anthropomorphic projection of the worst of human behavior. It later eats her and her grandmother, but eventually they are rescued after the wolf is killed. Recalling my own childhood memories of this fairy tale, I wondered whether many children became frightened of real wolves after hearing this story.

It seems to be a part of normal human nature to ascribe undesirable characteristics to other groups, tribes, or nations. Demagogues through-

*Figure 1. In medieval Europe the evil image of the wolf was perpetuated and exploited for religious and political purposes.*

out history have exploited this trait to whip up hatred against their neighbors. It is not surprising, then, that we treat the wolf the same way by projecting onto it many of our own undesirable traits. According to Lopez, the medieval Roman Church, which dominated the daily lives of people in Europe, exploited the sinister image of the wolf (Figure 1) in order to create a sense of real devils prowling in the darkness. In his view, the Church sought to suppress social and political unrest by flushing out "werewolves" and putting them to death. Although the idea of werewolves goes back to ancient Greece, it flourished in medieval Europe, where the wolf had become a widespread symbol of evil. Lopez reports that thousands of men, women, and children were tried as werewolves and executed—often by burning alive. By equating fellow humans with the hated wolves, people could see themselves as better and

79

thus purge themselves of the evil in their own nature by assigning it to something outside of themselves. Even today we refer to a very sadistic murderer or rapist as "that animal," when in fact the behavior is distinctly human.

Seeing the wolf as a part of nature in its own right never made much headway in medieval times. However, it is reported that St. Francis, in keeping with his humane attitude toward all living things, made a pact with a wolf in Gubbio, Italy, to have it desist from threatening the villagers in return for being fed and allowed to wander freely through the town (Lopez 1978).

# Man and Wolf as Competitors

Early European pastoralists and farmers probably knew very little about the ways of the wolves with which they shared a common habitat, other than that wolves killed their livestock. The wolf thus became hated as a raider and an enemy, and to this day ranchers chiefly see what (to them) is the bad side of the wolf—its predatory nature.

Also, human hunters and wolves have always been considered to be competitors for the same food resources. North American Indians and Eskimos never complained much about this competition, and seem not to have begrudged the wolf its share of nature's bounty. In fact, native human hunters ascribed to wolves many positive qualities such as intelligence, boldness, and skill. Their knowledge of wolf behavior in a natural setting contrasts with that of European peasants and city dwellers, who rarely changed their attitudes after arriving in North America. Among the rare exceptions to this rule is Stefansson, an Arctic explorer and scientist who regarded the wolf as just another inhabitant of the northern wilderness. In his book *The Friendly Arctic* (1921), the only real problem with wolves he describes is having to protect his food caches from them. He never killed wolves for raiding his caches, and never had the hatred for predators which characterized the attitudes of the majority of European descendants in North America.

# Wolf and Human Nature Compared

The similarity between human and wolf social organization has frequently been noted (see Hall and Sharp 1978). Many early human groups, such a certain Indian and Eskimo peoples of North America, hunted in small groups similar to wolf packs, with one or more high-ranking group members acting as hunt leaders. Among these native peoples there is evidence of territorial behavior in the form of dividing up the hunting range among groups. Perhaps most significant, it is this similarity of the human social structure to wolf social organization that, thousands of years ago, permitted the successful domestication of the early ancestors of today's dogs. Breeding for selected characteristics has produced dogs that not only work for us but enjoy human companionship as a substitute for the pack. (See Fox 1978, and Scott and Fuller 1965 for additional information on the differences between dogs and wolves and their common ancestry.)

# Exaggerated Wolf Deeds

People have vivid imaginations that fill the gaps in their factual knowledge. Fueled by fear, rumors spread, and sometimes panic results. This is as true today as it was centuries ago, and it seems to be the reason why the wolf was, and still is, so little understood by the public and so greatly feared.

In North America, an important reason for the exaggeration of the negative behavior of wolves is the bounty system. Inappropriate animal-husbandry practices brought here from other countries led to the loss of many domesticated animals. Wolves did take their share of livestock, especially when human activities displaced or destroyed their natural prey, but because they were the most easily identified cause of the losses, they got more than their share of the blame. The clamor to compensate livestock owners gave rise to a bounty system, and the need to rally political support for such a system led to exaggerations of danger and losses. In the absence of factual data to counteract outrageous stories

81

about wolves, bounty payments were deemed justified. Abuses of the system were numerous, and bounties could be paid several times over for the same animal, since the ears might be required as evidence in one county while the tail sufficed in another (see Lopez 1978; Brown 1983).

A final reason for exaggerations about wolf behavior was probably the attention and admiration which the horror stories brought to the teller from those sitting around the potbellied stove in the local store, or from the grandchildren in grandfather's lap at storytelling time.

## The Objective Basis for the Fear of Wolves

Present-day wolf lovers sometimes give the impression that all negative reports about wolves are exaggerated, if not totally invented. A more critical evalation of wolf behavior, however, shows that there are a considerable number of facts which may underlie historical and recent wolflore.

The sight of wolves killing and eating animals can be very unpleasant to many people. And when the victims are livestock owned and tended by a witness who often knows the individual animals being killed, identification with them—perhaps as social companions—elicits anger, frustration, and even hatred. On the outskirts of Fairbanks, Alaska, and in rural Minnesota, wolves have reportedly killed and eaten peoples' dogs in front of children waiting for school buses. The fact is that such killings do occur, and they do nothing to endear the wolf to the dogs' owners and their neighbors. Furthermore, how do these residents know, indeed how do scientists know, that the children themselves are really safe? In Los Angeles a free-living coyote pack killed a young girl in broad daylight; might not wolves do the same? The literature on wild North American wolves strongly suggests that they do not attack humans, even when provoked. Russell and Pimlott (1968) described an investigation of up to ninety claims of wolf attacks on humans in Ontario, Canada. All but one did not stand up "to investigation," and in the one attack that was fairly well documented, the wolf was very likely rabid.

While rabies is rare in wild wolves in North America, it does occur. In different regions of the United States the disease is endemic in raccoons, skunks, foxes, and other wild animals. Chapman (1978) reported that during his observations of a wild wolf pack in the Brooks Range in Alaska, one wolf became rabid and he had to shoot it. Within a short time the entire pack was wiped out by the disease, which checked its further spread. There may have been other instances that were not written up. True, the problem is statistically insignificant, but like the fear of rabid bats—where there is an equally low probability of being bitten—it is based on a fact or two. Is it reasonable to expect a nonbiologist to have the confidence of the professional wildlife researcher in assessing the danger? Two interesting stories will highlight this difference between nonprofessional and the professional.

A few years ago I was informed of a wolf attack on a hunter and his son. Apparently they were approaching a rendezvous site where some almost adult-sized wolf pups were awaiting the return of the pack from a hunt. The pups must have mistaken the men for pack members and came bounding out of the bushes to meet them. The father, finding himself and his son face to face with about seven wolves, dropped to his knees and shot five of them, while the rest disappeared into the bush.

Later that same year, Dr. David Mech of the U.S. Fish and Wildlife Service and Fred Harrington, a graduate student, were in a similar situation. When they approached a known rendezvous site in Minnesota, the pups heard them and came running toward them on the path. Knowing wolves, Mech said, "Let's wait and see how long it takes them to figure out that we are not the returning pack." The wolves came quite close before they realized their mistake and fled into the bush (Mech, pers. comm.). It would be nice if all hunters knew what David Mech knows about wolves. While we can regret the deaths of those innocent wolf pups, can we really blame the father for shooting them when he *thought* he and his son were being attacked?

## Positive Perspectives

Prior to the scientific study of the behavior and ecology of wolves, few good things were said about them. However, in recounting the oral history of pre-Oneida Indians in North America, Paula Underwood Spencer

83

(1983) tells of the realistic and respectful attitude these people had toward the wolves with whom they shared the land. And Lopez (1978) recalls wolf stories of the Blackfeet, Pawnee, and Cheyenne Indians that cast the wolf in a positive light. He recounts one story, recorded by George Bird Grinnell, called "Black Wolf and His Fathers," in which a man left to die in a pit is rescued by two wolves—one white and one rabid. During their journey to the Place of the Wolves the white wolf guards the man against the rabid one, and with the white wolf's help the man is adopted by the pack. When the man returns to his tribe he kills the two women who left him in the pit and offers their bodies to the wolves. And finally, there is of course the legend of Romulus and Remus, the founders of Rome, who were said to have been nursed by a wolf, and Kipling's Mowgli, who was reared by wolves.

Within the last few years some newspaper reports from Europe and Russia have described positive characteristics of wolves. For instance, a little girl was lost in a snow storm, and found the next morning in good health. She reported that a big dog had curled around her and kept her warm. The tracks in the snow were said to be those of a wolf.

Workers along the Alaskan pipeline used to feed wolves despite strict orders not to. The wolves soon learned that there was food to be had at the workers' camps, and they often chased pickup trucks from which workers tossed sandwiches. In one instance a timid wolf snatched some food from one man's hand and got part of a finger as well.

# Changing Perceptions of the Wolf

## Increasing Public Understanding of Wolf Behavior

Scientific studies of the ecology and behavior of wolves began in the early 1940s (Young and Goldman 1944, Murie 1944, Schenkel 1947). The social relationships of a group of wolves at Chicago's Brookfield Zoological Park were described in great detail by Rabb, Woolpy, and Ginsburg (1967).

Long-term studies of wild wolves began in 1957 on Isle Royale in Lake Superior. The first results were published by Mech (1966), and this work was soon followed by a comprehensive ecological and behavioral synthesis, *The Wolf* (Mech 1970). The research carried out on Isle Royale over the last two decades has been summarized by Allen (1979) in *The Wolves of Minong*.

This body of research on wolves has brought much favorable attention to the species in scientific and academic circles, but credit for changing public attitudes about the wolf is due first of all to writers of popular books who have had, beyond doubt, a greater impact on the general public than biologists have. Farley Mowat had such an impact with his book *Never Cry Wolf* (1963), in which he wrote about his stay in the Canadian wilderness while on assignment as a Canadian government biologist. His job was to find the reason for the decline of the caribou population, which had been blamed on wolves. Mowat found instead that wanton slaughter by native humans had decimated the herds. I have found that more people have first become interested in wolves through his book than from any other source. It has now been made into a well-received movie, also called "Never Cry Wolf," so his message has reached an even larger audience.

Documentary films about humans hunting wolves and the behavior of wolves in the wild and in captivity have also increased our understanding and appreciation of wolves. Some of the best of these films are "Wolfmen," "Death of a Legend," and "Tundra Wolves."

Although most people get to see wolves only in films or on television, there are still a few opportunities to see live wolves. Many zoos, like the National Zoo in Washington, D.C., exhibit them. There are also, in several locations around the country, wolf breeding and research centers that also exhibit wolves for the public to see. Wolf Park in Battle Ground, Indiana, which I founded in 1972, is one such center. At Wolf Park visitors can see wolves in a packlike group and learn about wild and captive wolves.

Never has the wolf gotten such good press as it does now (Figure 2). Public pressure in the United States and Canada is now strong enough to win out in many instances against ill-conceived control or extermination campaigns against the wolf. The wolf has even come under the protection of the courts: On January 5, 1984, in the U.S. District Court in Minne-

*Figure 2. The wolf is now seen in a more positive way by an increasing number of people in the United States. Favorable treatment of wolves in popular books and films has contributed to this new perception. (Illustration by Sally Bensusen.)*

sota, Judge Miles Lord rejected a plan by the U.S. Fish and Wildlife Service to place wolf management in the hands of the Minnesota Department of Natural Resources. This plan would have opened the way for legal trapping and sport hunting of wolves. The U.S. Fish and Wildlife Service receives more mail on pending wolf legislation and regulations than on any other endangered species. This concern is not only with the wolf as a unique animal, but with the wolf as a symbol of the vanishing wilderness in North America.

## The New Mythology about the Wolf

While some people still oppose and even despise the wolf, a significant number in the United States and Canada now have such a favorable image that in their eyes it can do no wrong. As these people see it, anything that the wolf does naturally is all right. When a wolf kills, that is as it should be. While they rightly deplore the suffering of a wolf in a trap, they have no compassion for a moose that is brought down and eaten alive. Some people go so far as to deny that wolves actually kill and eat sheep and other livestock, and I have heard it suggested in all seriousness that if the people in Minnesota don't like wolves they should just move away.

Many wolf sympathizers understand its role in the wild and its relationship to its prey. However, there are others who fail to appreciate that unchecked wolf populations will expand and inevitably come into conflict with humans and livestock. They are unable to accept that some wolves might have to die to safeguard human interests. They seriously suggest that offending wolves be trapped in Minnesota and sent elsewhere, without regard to the problems that this may create for the people elsewhere, as well as for the transplanted wolves themselves. And some of these people even have the romantic notion that if they love a wolf, the wolf should love them in return. They are actually offended when a tame wolf ignores them, or even snaps or growls at them.

There seem to be two main reasons underlying this new mythology about the wolf: One is a wholly anthropomorphic attitude toward the animal, fostered by a lack of appreciation for the differences between dogs and wolves; and the second is a genuine love for animals coupled with a sense of justice born of revulsion at what people have done and are still doing to wolves. While this pro-wolf sentiment is understandable, and often translates into lobbying support for protective legislation, it also affects the credibility of wolf supporters, which is essential in winning the cooperation of the people on whose land wild wolves live.

## Wolves and Wolf–Dog Hybrids as Pets

For many people, personal contact with a wolf can bring back a feeling most of us modern humans lost when we transformed the wilderness and lost touch with nature. For them, owning a wolf can be both a substitute for the lost natural world and a challenge: To be master of a wolf means to control something wild and wonderful. Owning a wolf also enhances the owner's self-esteem, and often wins him admiration in the eyes of others. And for some men, a pet wolf represents a macho symbol that they can show off to their peers.

Very few people really know much about wolves. Some people will buy a wolf, paying from $300 to $600, perhaps up to $1,000 for a white one. Eventually a number of buyers will have second thoughts about their purchases. During the last seven years, over 190 pet wolves have been offered to Wolf Park by people who no longer wanted them, or who could no longer keep them because the neighbors complained about the howling, or because they killed the neighbor's cat or bit someone.

Wolf–dog hybrids are another matter. While many are kept properly and seem to make fine pets, many uninformed individuals raise them solely for the money and do not take the care that one would expect from responsible breeders to raise them under proper conditions. Furthermore, regardless of the source, wolves and wolf–dog hybrids have one important flaw as pets: Even if they are well socialized and friendly to humans, their hunting instinct cannot be totally eliminated by early handling experiences. As a result, the proper stimulus situation, such as a crying, running, or stumbling child, may trigger an attack. Tame wolves—unlike their wild brethren—are often involved in such incidents, and so are an increasing number of wolf–dog hybrids across the country.

In my judgment, people should not keep wolves as pets. However, if they cannot be deterred legally—as is still true in most states—people who want to keep wolves owe it to the animals to provide them with certain minimum conditions. First of all, they should have at least two wolves, since no human can properly fulfill all of a wolf's social needs. Wolves should be fed raw meat and carcasses, not dog food, and they should have a big and secure place to run in. There should be a high fence with an overhang; the bottom of the fence should either be deep in the ground or have a wire apron inside on the ground. They should be able to dig, howl, and be *wolves* in addition to being companions to humans. Finally, they should be kept in a place where neighbors will not object, and they should be so fenced that no unsuspecting child can reach through the fence and have its hand bitten and torn.

# The Wolf's Future in North America

European immigrants to North America brought along their negative attitudes toward the wolf, and this resulted in efforts to destroy wolves wherever they were found. As the continent was settled during the westward migration, the wolf and one of its prey species, the American bison, had to give way.

Today, large enough wilderness areas have survived to provide refuge for the wolf and its prey. Beginning about forty years ago, popular and scientific study has brought about a new understanding of the wolf that has dispelled many of the earlier myths that misrepresented the wolf to its detriment. Active wolf management plans now exist under the auspices of the U.S. Fish and Wildlife Service, which has created conservation programs for the Eastern timberwolf, the Rocky Mountain grey wolf, the Mexican wolf, and the red wolf. Even in Mexico, where only a few wild wolves survive, efforts are underway to protect the few that are left, and a special program has been initiated to perpetuate the Mexican subspecies in captivity for possible release of animals into suitable habitat in the wild. In Canada, each individual province is responsible for the management of its own wolf population. This often includes controversial local programs, which, as in the U.S., are designed to control, not exterminate, the wolf.

Today what most endangers the wolf in North America is the constant expansion of human activities into its wilderness habitat. The exploitation of oil and mineral resources and the accompanying expansion of human settlements, or any other activity that adversely affects prey populations, soon lead to a decline in wolves. In regions of Superior National Forest in Minnesota, wolf numbers depend upon the availability of deer. Human hunting, a maturing forest, and hard winters all contribute to the decline of deer numbers, which in turn affects the wolf population (Nelson and Mech 1981). In general, however, the wolf seems fairly secure in its present range for the foreseeable future. There has even been a migration of wolves from Minnesota into the northern part of Wisconsin. These wolves are closely monitored and protected, and no wolf control in farm areas has as yet been necessary (Thiel 1983).

# Conclusion

The wolf has become a symbol of the vanishing wilderness for many people in North America. Its controversial nature has provided the impetus for scientific study, and the relentless and cruel persecutions of the past, combined with more accurate information about the wolf, have created a backlash that has resulted in protective legislation and led to an increasing public awareness of the value of the wolf in the wild. The past and present enmity toward the wolf in the attitudes of many Americans, Canadians, and Mexicans is now confronted by a growing number of people whose attitudes are more like those of the Indians and Eskimos who for so long lived symbiotically with the wolf. These people do recognize the wolf as a predator and accept the need to kill individual wolves to protect livestock. However, they are also aware that both scientific methods and old-fashioned techniques like livestock-guarding dogs can be used to manage the wolf intelligently and humanely. Wolf sympathizers want these remarkable animals left alone when there is no conflict with livestock.

# Select Bibliography

Allen, D. 1979. *The wolves of Minong*. New York: Houghton Mifflin Co.

Brown, D.E., ed. 1983. *The wolf in the Southwest*. Tucson: University of Arizona Press.

Chapman, R.C. 1978. Rabies: Decimation of a wolf pack in arctic Alaska. *Science* vol. 201:365–67.

Fox, M.W. 1978. *The dog—Its domestication and behavior*. New York: Garland STPM Press.

Hall, R.L., and H.S. Sharp. 1978. *Wolf and man: Evolution in parallel*. New York: Academic Press.

Lopez, B.H. 1978. *Of wolves and men*. New York: Charles Scribner's Sons.

Mech, L.D. 1966. *The wolves of Isle Royale*. Fauna of the National Parks of the United Series, Fauna Series 7. Washington, D.C.: U.S. Government Printing Office.

————. 1970. *The wolf*. Garden City, N.Y.: The Natural History Press. Reprinted 1981. Minneapolis: University of Minnesota Press.

Mowat, F. 1963. *Never cry wolf*. New York: Dell Publishing.

Murie, A. 1944. *The wolves of Mount McKinley*. U.S. Department of the Interior, National Park Service, Fauna Series 5. Washington, D.C.: U.S. Government Printing Office.

Nelson, M.E., and L.D. Mech. 1981. Deer social organization and wolf predation in Northeastern Minnesota. In *Wildlife monographs*, no. 77.

Rabb, G.B., J.H. Woolpy, and B.E. Ginsburg. 1967. Social relationships in a group of captive wolves. *American Zoologist* 7:305–11.

Rutter, J.J., and D.H. Pimlott. 1968. *The world of the wolf.* Philadelphia and New York: J.B. Lippincott Co.

Schenkel, R. 1947. Expression studies of wolves, trans. A. Klasson. *Behavior* 1:81–129.

Scott, J.P., and J.L. Fuller. 1965. *Genetics and social behavior of the dog.* Chicago: University of Chicago Press.

Spencer, P.U. 1983. *Who speaks for wolf.* Austin, TX: Tribe of Two Press.

Stefansson, V. 1921. *The friendly Arctic.* New York: Macmillan Co.

Thiel, R.P. 1983. Field Progress Report No. 5. State of Wisconsin: Department of Natural Resources.

Young, S.P., and E.A. Goldman. 1944. *The wolves of North America.* Washington, D.C.: American Wildlife Institute. Reprinted 1964. New York: Dover Publications, Inc.

Zimen, E. 1981. *The wolf.* New York: Delacorte Press.

# Self-imaging and Animals in TV Ads

**JoAnn Magdoff and Steve Barnett**

A cat cha-chas across boxes of cat food to the beat of "chow, chow, chow," delighting the motherly woman feeding it. In the mid-1980s this TV ad was the spot most recalled and most discussed by TV viewers when asked to name a commercial that included an animal. Why was this ad so popular? Was it nothing more than the cuteness of the syncopated editing of the cat's movements? Are animals in TV commercials simply easy vehicles for humor and sustained viewer interest? In a research project on how viewers perceive animals in TV advertising, we discovered that animals are more than that—they are used in subtle ways that link product identification with differing female and male self-images.

# Animals as Evocative Images

The use of animals, both animated and real, in many TV ads is directly related to the ability of the animals to evoke powerful responses in viewers—animals become "as-if" representations of the viewer's idealized self-image, in terms of both positive attributes and desired relationships. Animals are particularly appropriate male and female symbols to Americans because, unlike people in some other societies, Americans tend to believe that animals, especially mammals, have families similar to human families. Pets are often seen as members of the family. Animals are also important symbols for advertisers because Americans tend to believe that certain attributes are characteristic of certain kinds of animals: Owls are wise, cats are finicky, and so on. The fastest way to make a point in a TV spot is to use a visual image whose meaning viewers agree upon. Using stereotypical animals in commercials is a standard tactic; animals are anthropomorphized and often animated to emphasize one essential product characteristic. Like characters in folklore or cartoons, animals may typify a single "human" characteristic or be a recognizable type—for example, the owl representing Wise potato chips in TV spots and on the package. Animals also can easily represent paired opposites basic to our ideas of self and other, like tame/wild, lovable/dangerous, powerful/weak, dominant/submissive, and playful/austere.

# Gender Differences in Human Responses to Animal Images

By combining psychological and anthropological methods, we discovered that men and women respond differently to the animals they see in TV ads. For women, animals primarily represent nurturant relations, while for men, animals tend to embody desirable attributes. But we also discovered some developing trends that reflect how gender-specific roles are being transformed in our culture.

Across the country we showed TV ads involving animals to 230 adults—130 women and 100 men—who were representative of the demo-

*Figure 1. In marketing cat food, advertisers promote cats as members of the family, a practice that appears to be well received by the American public. (Illustration by Sally Bensusen.)*

graphics for the United States in income, age, education, and ethnicity. At each session participants were asked to discuss among themselves what they thought the ads meant, whom the ads appealed to, and their own personal reaction to the ads. Our goal was to let participants freely discuss animals in TV ads, using their own language and expressing their own feelings. In addition, participants were given a psychological questionnaire on self-image and relationships with family and friends. We then analyzed participant reactions to the ads in light of their psychological profiles. The project was limited to animals in automobile, beer, and cat and dog food spots, since animals figure prominently in these product categories.

All our respondents considered cats notoriously finicky eaters: Once they have tasted cream, they won't drink milk; once they've eaten tuna, it's goodbye to dry cat food. In cat food commercials, it seems, although the cat is a cat, it also is a member of the family (Figure 1). The identification is through a relationship: Finicky cat is to cat food as finicky child or husband is to human food. Both the finicky cat and the child or husband can be cajoled or tricked out of finickiness by someone who knows the right way to feed it. The way to get all three finicky eaters to eat happily is to cajole, entice, and playfully seduce. Animal food commercials are typically aimed at women-as-mothers, for it is mostly Mommy who buys and prepares the food for cats, dogs, children, and Daddy. Watching a cat food commercial, one woman respondent said, "That's exactly how I get my husband to eat salad." Where men are shown in cat food commercials, typically they are prissy, older bachelors in bow ties presented as "old maids."

Car ads using images of wild cats like cheetahs, panthers, and so on were positively received by most male respondents. The men in the ads are clearly in the driver's seat—rugged, tough men of action. They are perceived as strong, fast, in charge, controlling the animal's wildness. Domestic cats are like members of the family; wild cats are powerful but controllable, as in the old Exxon commercials ("Put a tiger in your tank").

Dog food spots can show hearty outdoorsmen, since "real men" may have nurturant relations with dogs, if not with cats. In dog food ads directed at men, dogs illustrate desirable male attributes like bravery, spirit, and loyalty (Figure 2).

Women, on the other hand, do not identify primarily with the product or with the product's attributes, but rather with the results of having bought and dispensed the product. The satisfaction of others demonstrates their own superior style of nurturance. Women are involved in relationships with product and family, especially nurturing relationships. Female respondents, particularly housewives, talked extensively about the gratification they felt when husband, children, and pets ate well: "I love it when my baby smiles after a meal," said one. "I love it when my cat licks her lips after a meal," said another.

In contrast, men "go for it" themselves. They are sold psychological identification with attributes symbolized by animals rather than identification with relationships. Unlike women and cat food, men and beer/cars/gasoline/and so on are identified with the product's attributes. Think of the bull in Schlitz Malt Liquor ads (out of control, dangerous), and the bull in Merrill Lynch stock brokerage ads (precise, in exquisite control). Both appeal to men: the former as being able to handle the danger, the latter as being in control of potentially enormous power.

*Figure 2. When men are the targets of dog food ads, dogs are portrayed in ways that illustrate desirable male attributes like bravery, spirit, and loyalty. (Illustration by Sally Bensusen.)*

In car commercials, wild cats are intercut with sexy, anything-but-domestic women who are iconographic feline representations. Although the leopard prowling around the car may share some attributes with the woman draped over it, the qualities of the big cats in car commercials are not primarily metaphorical. The car contains the leopard's power, grace, and wildness. The man who drives it assumes these attributes and will attract the sensuality, grace, and wildness of the woman. The car then becomes the means by which the leopard and the woman get to be related to the man, not by analogy or metaphor, but by an incorporative identification. The man is in the driver's seat—the aggression and sexuality of the cat and woman are embodied in the car, and *he* is driving—almost taming the desirably wild, almost losing control to the thrillingly dangerous. Male respondents easily discussed the attributes of the cat (power, grace, explosiveness) as attributes of the car, its gasoline (especially if it is Exxon's "tiger in your tank"), and ultimately of themselves, and simultaneously felt excited and nervous about being able to control the sexy women appearing in some car ads.

The Budweiser Clydesdale horse is another important symbol of desired male attributes. In the spot we showed respondents, there is a relay race among several two-man teams. The ad follows one team in which each individual is running hard. Their strides are intercut with the galloping Budweiser horse, with background music evoking the popular British film about Olympic runners, "Chariots of Fire." The horse combines its own vitality with the men's energy. The horse's power is like the power of the running men, and the message makes a powerful attributional statement: If you drink Budweiser, you will take on the strength, vitality, and virility of the horse. As one male respondent said, "The horse feels like a powerful runner and that's how I feel watching it." But horses can be symbolically understood in two ways. Like the panther in the car commercial, they are wild; like the house cats in the cat food commercials, they can be tamed. The implication here is that man, like the horse, is both wild and, if not fully domesticated, at least tameable. As another male respondent said, "You never can tell with a horse; you think you have him under control and he runs wild; that's how I tell my wife to think about me."

So far we have suggested a clear difference between animal symbols directed toward men and women:

> For women, animals primarily express relationships;
> For men, animals primarily embody desirable attributes.

Of course, there were exceptions to these generalizations. Men who scored high on nurturant qualities tended to respond more positively to relational ads, while women who scored high on autonomy tended to respond more positively to attributional ads. But when we divided animal ads into those stressing relationships and those stressing attributes, 72 percent of respondents said that relational ads were directed at women, and 80 percent said attributional ads were directed at men.

# The Changing Response of Women

This solid and consistent difference between the sexes, however—like so many others—appears to be changing. Recent ads show an innovative use of animals to express changing female self-imaging. The most talked-about advertisement in our research was the cleverly-edited cat food spot in which a cat appears to do a demure, ladylike cha-cha in time to the refrain of "chow, chow, chow." Many female respondents felt that they were being appealed to in this commercial not merely as nurturers of others, but as a sexy, kittenish cat. The dancing cat was like themselves, unrelated to a child or husband. One woman said, "I sometimes dance like that when I'm alone in the house doing things that make me feel good." Women are still nurturers, but now they are feeding the cat as a way to feed the sexy, kittenish parts of themselves. So also for perfume print ads directed at women: Where a wild cat or snake is presented, it represents female sensuality. Fifty percent of younger working women in our sample responded positively to attributional ads, versus only 18 percent of older women, who were mostly housewives. Like men, women are beginning to assume the attributes of the animal, although these attributes are still gender-specific: female sexy-as-kittenish vs. male sexy-as-commanding.

But perhaps the "cha-cha-cha" of the Purina cat expresses more than just a new willingness of women to identify with nontraditional roles. Perhaps it expresses an important kernel within the egocentrism of the "me decade." Stripping away the just-plain-selfish aspects of the "new" emphasis on self, we are left with a burgeoning, if hesitantly expressed, notion of *entitlement*—the idea that, by virtue of self-acceptance, one deserves certain benefits and rewards. "Entitlement" has come to mean an inalienable psychological right—a statement of what we deserve, a mark of justifiable self-esteem. It is not only linked to specifics, it is a stance toward the world.

We suggest that the "chow, chow, chow" spot is the beginning of an expression of entitlement for a segment of the population long targeted by advertisers and long neglected as autonomous individuals—mothers and housewives. Marketing to women on the basis of identifying with attri-

99

butes is not new—it has been used before to sell perfume and clothing. However, the Purina dancing cat commercial is the first one in which the woman is performing traditional tasks as housewife, mother, and nurturer and yet is simultaneously identified with something sexy, albeit in a refined, low-keyed, respectable way. The symbolic forms used in the past to sell on the basis of attributes, which have been associated with men or with obviously nubile and single women, are being used in the Purina spot to sell to women as mothers.

We found that female respondents who scored high in feelings of autonomy, entitlement, and self-esteem also tended to respond more positively to animals in male-oriented ads, as well as to the "chow, chow, chow" ad. Sixty-eight percent of female respondents who are mothers with high feelings of entitlement and self-esteem responded positively to the attributional aspects of the Purina ad (saw aspects of themselves in the dancing cat), while only 32 percent of low-entitlement and low-self-esteem mothers did. The punch of the commercial—why it is the first one respondents mentioned—may well be that the sense of entitlement and of self which it presents through attributional self-imaging does not interfere with a woman's nurturant role, but rather enhances her as a person. The spot endorses personal wholeness and a comfortable, entitled sense of autonomy of selfhood that need not interfere with one's role and self-esteem as a nurturer. The symbolism of the cat conveys all of this in an unthreatening way.

# Conclusion

Animals can signify many things: family roles, wildness, unpredictability, power, sexiness. They can signify relationships, attributes, or both. This is what makes them so effective in ads focusing on gender-specific roles. It now appears that the depiction of animals in TV commercials is slowly changing along with the changing notions of gender and self in our culture. As our own self-images change, the animal images we choose to reflect ourselves change along with them.

# The Horse: Noble Steed or Wild Menace?

**Joel Berger**

More than forty-five thousand books have been written about horses—probably more than have been published on any other mammal except for man and the dog. Not only are horses ubiquitous, but their appearance in historical writings, mythology, and art, and their use in exploration, war, sports, leisure, farming, and other work, are testimony to their enduring popularity. Thus it is perplexing that when horses live in the wild, without the constraints of man, they often are no longer lauded as noble steeds, but are instead considered wild menaces. In some Australian districts, it is still legal to shoot feral horses, and only within the past two decades has legislation been enacted in the United States to protect them.

It is my aim in this chapter to present the horse in historical perspective, to review the varied and complex relationships that have developed between humans and horses, and finally to explore the current controversies that have developed as a result of the flourishing populations of horses that have been introduced into new environments. In addressing the last point, I will look at horses in the American West and point out that to understand horses as wild animals one must study them within the context of their ecological setting.

# The Evolution of the Horse

The earliest horse was a small, cat-sized animal that roamed the then-moist, tropical-like forests of Europe and North America about fifty-five to sixty million years ago. *Hyracotherium*, as the fossil is called by paleontologists, was an herbivore that gave rise to a variety of species, several of which adapted to the savannas and grasslands that spread across North America about twenty million years ago. Some of these early North American horses were the direct ancestors of the modern genus *Equus*. It was from these ancestors that modern species of horses, all members of the family Equidae, arose.

Many equids appear to have left North America by crossing the Bering land bridge in numerous waves, successfully colonizing Asia, Europe, and Africa. These continents proved to be the salvation of equids, because in North America horses (and numerous other large mammals including rhinos, mammoths, and camels) became extinct within the last fifteen thousand years. Today, however, only six species of wild equids remain, a small remnant of a formerly more successful group. These species are Grevy's zebras, plains zebras, mountain zebras, onagers, asses, and Przewalski's horses.

Przewalski's horses, also known as Mongolian wild horses, are the only true wild horses. Unfortunately, they are extinct in their native habitats and exist only in small, inbred zoo populations. They, or some very closely related species, were the ancestors of the domesticated horses we know today. The horses that will later be referred to as wild are actually feral—domesticated animals that escaped from man and survive without human assistance.

# The Status of the Horse in Human Culture

## Horses in Early Cultures

It is not clear where horses were first domesticated, but it is well known that they played an important role in ancient cultures. Horses were revered in early Greece and Rome as animals of beauty, strength, and valor, and were frequently depicted in sculpture. They were used to pull chariots and became part of sporting events (Figure 1), and they played prominent roles in Greek and Roman militias; it is even said that Philip of Macedon seized twenty thousand horses from the Scythians, most probably for military purposes (Clutton-Brock 1981).

*Figure 1. The pulling of chariots was one of the early uses of domesticated horses.*
*Horse-drawn chariots are depicted in the artwork of many ancient civilizations of the*
*eastern Mediterranean.*

In Eurasia, documentation of the origins and uses of horses is fragmentary. It appears that certain nomadic cultures of the southern Ukraine first domesticated horses as a dependable food source and as draft animals as early as 3500 B.C.; the riding of horses first appeared in Mesopotamia just before 2000 B.C. (Bökönyi 1984).

## Horses in Western Mythology and Art

Since horses were so important in early European and Middle Eastern cultures, it is not surprising that they were highly regarded and well represented in Western mythology and art. Throughout history, horses were granted divine status and became symbols of the gods. Pegasus, the winged steed of Greek mythology, later became the name for a constellation. Another famed mythical creature, the Centaur, was half man and half horse. Paintings and sculpture from many periods of European history depict kings, warriors, and other important people astride their horses. Medieval European tapestries are filled with unicorns; it was believed that the unicorn's spiral horn had magical properties. Only with the discovery of the narwhal, a rare marine mammal, by Martin Frobisher in the sixteenth century was it learned that the "elusive unicorn" did not really exist. Many other stories involving horses also found their way into historical literature. One of the best known is the story of Lady Godiva, unfortunate wife of a cruel and powerful man. The lady could get her husband to repeal his unfair taxes only if she rode naked on her noble horse through the streets of the town. It is clear that in Western mythology and art, the horse generally has been portrayed very favorably.

# Wild Horses in the Americas

There were no native horses left in the Americas when the first Europeans arrived. However, many of the horses that these immigrants brought with them went feral and established thriving populations. In South America, Charles Darwin observed horses on the pampas, and traced their origin to the introduction of horses to the Falkland Islands in the 1760s. Wild horses became widespread in South America, where they occurred in Argentina, Brazil, Chile, Peru, and Venezuela. In 1838, Don Felix de Azara commented on the problem of Paraguayan horses (Azara 1838:5):

> These wild horses congregate together everywhere in such immense herds, that it is no exaggeration to say, they sometimes amount to twelve thousand individuals. They are most troublesome and prejudicial; for, besides consuming vast quantities of pasture, they gallop up to the domesticated horses whenever they see them; and, passing amongst or close to them; call and caress them with low affectionate neighings . . . and easily induce them to incorporate within their troops.

Colonel Charles Hamilton Smith wrote in 1841 of the resiliency of wild horses (Smith 1841:474–75):

> The time is not perhaps far distant, when they will be gradually again absorbed by domestication, excepting those which will retreat toward the two poles; as the species is not restricted by the rigor of the climate, but solely by the extent of available foods, the wilds of Patagonia and the latitudes of the northern deserts will continue to maintain them in freedom.

Wild horses have survived handily in North America. Populations have existed for at least two hundred years on Sable Island, a fragmented chain of sand dunes situated in the North Atlantic, as well as on less remote islands such as Assateague and Shackleford Banks. However, it is not clear whether the horses that now live in these areas are descendants of the original Spanish horses that colonized North America. It is also uncertain whether horses of the American West derived originally from Hernando Cortez's 1519 landing near Vera Cruz, Mexico, or from Ferdinand (Hernando) de Soto's 1543 travels on the Mississippi River, or from animals that escaped more recently from ranchers. In any case, the horses that now run wild throughout the American West have existed in a feral state for many generations.

Estimates of the current population of feral horses in the American West vary tremendously. A 1982 census by the Bureau of Land Manage-

105

ment of the U.S. Department of the Interior reported a total population of about forty-five thousand, but a more recent National Research Council study suggests that this figure is conservative. In any case, it is clear that the number of wild horses has at least doubled and probably tripled since they became protected by law in 1917, with the greatest concentrations in the remote mountains of the Great Basin Desert, a sparsely populated area that includes most of Nevada and extensive parts of California and Utah. Although federal government roundups reduce some troublesome populations, the remaining abundance of horses still provokes controversy, and many people argue that better methods of containment are needed.

# Conservation Dilemmas

People who are concerned about conservation and ecology often express varying opinions about feral horses. Although many who hold horses in high regard favor their continued existence in the free-ranging state they have survived in for several centuries, others champion the removal of horses in order to return the ecosystem to a more "natural" condition. But can ecosystems that have been impaired by man now be repaired by removing horses? Probably not, considering the extent of other disruptive human activities such as mining, cattle grazing, and the introduction of exotic plants. The fundamental question of what impact horses have on Great Basin environments has yet to be answered, but there is evidence indicating that wild horses are not the culprits they are often alleged to be (Berger 1986). Below I will present evidence that horses do not compete directly with the large wildlife species of the Great Basin, and will explain why attempts to improve that ecosystem must contend with more than just horses.

## The Relative Abundance of Horses, Cattle, and Other Large Mammals

If one were to drive through the Great Basin on the interstate highways, the most common large mammals in sight would be cows and domestic horses. Wild horses occasionally wander down from the mountains in the winter, as do other large, native wild species of mammals such as pronghorn, mule deer, and bighorn sheep, but only in a few places can they be observed.

By comparing the combined body weights of the various species of ungulates in the Great Basin, it is possible to gain an idea of their relative abundances, and thus compare how much food each removes from the environment. The intuitively appealing alternative of comparing the total number of individuals of each species would be misleading, since one cow or horse does not require the same amount of food as one pronghorn or mule deer. Cows and horses are, on average, roughly eight to ten times the size of these native species, although the smaller species require a relatively greater proportion of food per unit of body weight. But the important point is that the biomass of introduced species in Nevada and western Utah clearly exceeds that of the native ones by at least an eighteen-fold magnitude (Figure 2). In fact, bighorn sheep and pronghorn, which were the most abundant species prior to European exploration and colonization of the Great Basin, now account for less than 1 percent of the total biomass. Feral horses contribute about 18 percent of the total biomass, while livestock (cattle, sheep, and goats) make up about 77 percent.

## Do Horses Compete with Native Ungulates?

Does the fact that species's biomasses are unequal necessarily imply that competition among species is occurring? For true competition to occur, two species must 1) use the same habitats; 2) exploit the same food or other resources; and 3) one species must depress the population size of the other. For Great Basin ungulates the appropriate information has never been collected systematically. Still, it is possible to gain some idea of the extent of competition through knowledge of the biology of the individual species.

Both cattle and horses feed primarily on grass, while mule deer and pronghorn rely on thick fibrous foods such as forbs (herbs other than grass) and browse. Although at times diets do overlap, for the most part wildlife biologists agree that the diets are sufficiently different to rule out

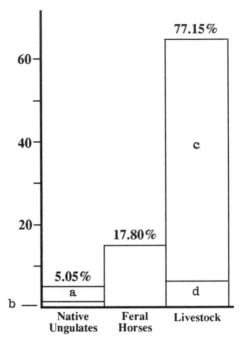

*Figure 2. Relationships between biomass and different categories of ungulates on public lands in the Great Basin Desert of Nevada and Utah in 1980 (standardized for 12 months of use). a = deer; b = bighorn, pronghorn; c = cattle; d = sheep, goats. (Adapted from Berger 1986.)*

direct competition for food. In fact, horses and cattle are much more likely to be in direct competition with each other than they are with mule deer or pronghorn. This potential competition for food is one of the main reasons why feral horses are so unpopular with ranchers.

Competition among cattle, horses, and bighorn sheep is more direct, since all three species consume grass. Wildlife biologists fear that unlimited grazing by cattle and horses could lead to the extermination of bighorn sheep. In very arid areas such as the Grand Canyon or Death Valley this could well be the case, and arguments about competition should be taken very seriously. However, in the northern Great Basin, where most feral horses occur, there are few bighorn sheep. Furthermore, bighorn sheep prefer the precipitous terrain of boulders and canyons, while cattle and horses rely on open, expansive shrub–steppe habitats (Figure 3). Under these circumstances it appears that, although food habits may be broadly similar, resources may be partitioned by differences in habitat preference. But this does not mean that nothing need be done in such cases. Wise management is always necessary to prevent introduced or exotic species from expanding into habitats preferred by native species and disrupting the equilibrium of the ecosystem.

So far I have suggested that little competition exists between native and exotic ungulates. But ecological relationships are not always straight-forward, and there is at least one case in which the introduction of an exotic species has actually helped a native species. Mule deer were relatively uncommon in the Great Basin when the first explorers visited the area, and only in the last one hundred years have their populations

*Figure 3. Feral horses are numerous in the American West; estimates of their population range from 45,000 to perhaps more than 100,000. Feral horses prefer wide-open steppe habitats to mountainous areas. (Illustration by Richard Swartz, derived from a photo provided by J. Berger.)*

prospered. Why did the advent of hordes of cattle and horses not decimate the mule deer habitats? It appears that by removing grasses, cattle and horses have promoted the growth of shrubs and forbs, important elements in the diet of mule deer (and pronghorn as well).

Unfortunately, although mule deer populations have increased, there has been an overall decline of bighorn sheep in most areas of the Great Basin, and pronghorn populations have been depleted to a mere fraction of their former levels. Although the introduction of domestic sheep in the late 1800s may have also introduced diseases, it is just as likely that a combination of factors, all stemming from the direct activities of man, resulted in the diminution of these native species. Regardless of the immediate reasons for the reduced numbers of some native species, a lack of concern for ecosystem dynamics and ecosystems in general has clearly resulted in the problems we now face. Feral horses might be a contributing factor in some cases, but they are not at the root of the problem.

## The Folly of the Wild Horse Controversy

Resource abuse in the Great Basin has probably been going on for more than one hundred years. Some of the more obvious problems include loss of native species of both plants and animals, declining water tables, salinization of topsoil, and unnaturally rapid erosion. Overgrazing can contribute significantly to these problems, and the reduction of introduced grazers is one step toward their alleviation. However, if we are interested in improving these ecosystems, we must do more than simply eliminate feral horses. Scientific principles of cattle grazing must also be implemented. Cattle negatively affect many habitats, particularly sensitive riparian (riverine) zones. A reduction in the number of cattle and horses will result in more grass but will in turn do little to solve other problems caused by mining, fencing off resources, poaching, off-road vehicles, and other forms of exploitative and recreational land use.

This is the folly of the wild horse controversy. If interest lies in the restoration of naturally functioning ecosystems, then introduced species should be removed and other measures taken to assure adequate protection of fragile regions. But the ecosystem cannot be restored by eliminating overgrazing without also taking into account man's other destructive activities. And when overgrazing is considered, it has to be analyzed in terms of the disproportionate influence of cattle. Sometimes economic interests must take precedence over others, but horses should not be declared the villain in deference to other, more abundant introduced animals without openly acknowledging that the real interests are economic. Management practices should follow sound scientific avenues and be designed to maximize gains in knowledge about interactions between all introduced species and their environments.

# Conclusion

For many centuries horses have been lauded and esteemed. These animals have aided humans in their varied conquests; horses have been celebrated in many different cultures, and have formed the economic basis for entire societies. I suspect that most people still view horses as noble beasts that symbolize glamor, beauty, and freedom.

Some people consider feral horses to be a menace because the dynamics of their ecosystems are poorly understood, and the confounding issues are often avoided. Feral horses cannot be studied apart from the complex ecosystems in which they exist. Surely it is worth the effort required to understand these noble animals and their relationship to habitat, native species, and agricultural economics in the American West before they are unnecessarily sacrificed.

# Select Bibliography

Azara, D.R. de. 1838. *The natural history of quadrupeds of Paraguay and the River La Plata., Vol. I.* Edinburgh: Adam and Charles Black.

Barclay, H.B. 1980. *The role of the horse in man's culture.* London: J.A. Allen.

Berger, J. 1986. *Wild horses of the Great Basin: Social competition and population size.* Chicago: University of Chicago Press.

Bökönyi, S. 1984. The horse. In *Evolution of domesticated animals*, ed. I.L. Mason. London: Longman.

Clark, K. 1977. *Animals and men*. London: Thames and Hudson.

Clutton-Brock, J. 1981. *Domesticated animals from early times*. London: The British Museum of Natural History and Heineman.

Dent, A. 1974. *The horse: Through fifty centuries of civilization*. London: Phaidon.

National Research Council. 1982. *Wild and free-roaming horses and burros*. Final report. Washington, D.C.: National Academy Press.

Ryden, H. 1970. *America's last wild horses*. New York: Ballantine.

Smith, C.H. 1841. *Horses: The naturalists library, Vol. 12*. Edinburgh: W.H. Lizars.

Thomas, H.S. 1979. *The wild horse controversy.* New Brunswick: Barnes and Co.

# How Companion Animals Make Us Feel

**Aaron Honori Katcher**

A full account of our awareness of the animals with which we live obviously is impossible. We can, however, profitably examine certain aspects of our relationships with animals and how they influence the way we think, talk, and feel. This chapter focuses on two feeling states that are consequences of contact with companion animals: safety and intimacy.

## Safety

### Physiological Responses to Aquarium Contemplation

In a series of studies, my colleagues and I focused on how the sight of undisturbed animal life can reduce our own level of arousal (Katcher *et*

*Figure 1. The contemplation of fish in an aquarium produces a relaxing effect on the human body, causing a reduction in blood pressure. (Illustration by Sally Bensusen.)*

*al.* 1983a; Katcher *et al.* 1984a, Katcher *et al.* 1984b). For these experiments, the major criteria for increased safety or relaxation were two physiological measures: decrease in heart rate and decrease in blood pressure. In all the experiments described, blood pressure (systolic, diastolic, and mean) and heart rate were measured, usually at one- or two-minute intervals, with an automated oscillometric monitor.

In our initial experiments, hypertensive and normal subjects sat quietly in a comfortable chair for twenty-five minutes (the equilibration period) to permit their blood pressures to reach a stable resting level, and were then asked to watch a tank stocked with a variety of common tropical fish (Figure 1). At three points in the experiment—prior to the equilibration period, and before and after the period of aquarium contemplation— subjects were asked to read aloud, so that the cardiovascular response to social interaction could be measured. Resting blood pressure fell and stabilized during the equilibration, and fell again as subjects watched the aquarium. Aquarium contemplation also decreased the arousal experienced when the subjects followed their aquarium contemplation by reading aloud.

In a subsequent investigation, we used a more complex experimental design to study the effect of aquarium contemplation on anxious subjects who were having dental surgery (i.e., one or more teeth extracted under local anaesthesia). Variables in the study included aquarium contemplation, hypnosis, and contemplation of a poster. Evaluations were conducted in pretreatment, and were not continued during surgery. Five conditions were studied: 1) aquarium contemplation alone; 2) aquarium contemplation used to initiate hypnotic relaxation; 3) contemplation of a poster; 4) contemplation of a poster combined with hypnotic induction; and 5) a control condition in which subjects were seated in a chair and simply told to relax. The patients' emotional response to the surgical procedure was measured with three independent methods: a patient questionnaire asking about his or her relative comfort and relaxation; a rating of the patient's overtly tense or anxious behavior during surgery by an observer; and the treating dentist's rating of the patient's level of relaxation and compliance during treatment. Both the dentist and the observer were kept in ignorance of the pretreatment condition for each subject.

In that study, all five procedures lowered blood pressure. All subjects who were hypnotized as well as those who contemplated the fish tank in their normal state of consciousness experienced more relaxation during surgery than the subjects who simply contemplated the poster or who were asked to "relax" without specific instructions (the control condition). The effect of poster contemplation alone was not significantly different from the control condition. On the patients' self-rating of emotional response, hypnosis and aquarium contemplation produced equivalent significant increases in relaxation (Figure 2). Furthermore, aquarium contemplation alone produced the maximum relaxation effect, so that the addition of hypnosis had no effect on those subjects contemplating the aquarium, but increased the amount of relaxation experienced by those subjects contemplating the poster to about the same level as those contemplating the

**PATIENT COMFORT INDEX**

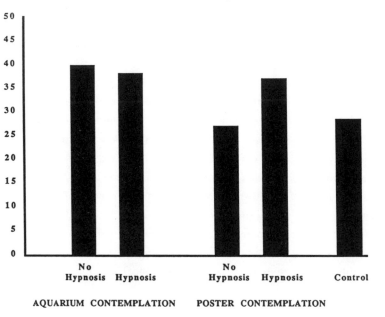

AQUARIUM CONTEMPLATION    POSTER CONTEMPLATION

*Figure 2. Effects of hypnosis and contemplation of aquarium and poster as reflected on a patient comfort index. The comfort index was derived from patients' ratings. Higher values equal more comfort and relaxation.*

aquarium. The same trends were present in the other two measures of patient response.

These results can be explained, in part, by the shift in attention produced by contemplation of the aquarium. When the subject's attention was directed at the aquarium, it became more difficult to think about the impending surgical procedure. Under experimental conditions, interruption of internal data processing by focusing attention on external stimuli results in a decrease in arousal (Lacey et al. 1963). This interruption of thought by a shift in attention is the best explanation for the decreased arousal observed with meditation and the relaxation response (Benson 1980). Hypnotic relaxation also fixes attention either on defined external stimuli or on the hypnotist's presence. Anxious subjects were not able to concentrate on the poster unless their ability to focus their attention was increased by hypnosis. The aquarium, however, was able to hold the attention of these anxious subjects, and hypnosis produced no additional effect.

The simplest interpretation of our experimental results is that an aquarium may be one of a whole series of effective distracters that include objects or sets of objects that move. However, I would like to advance the hypothesis that the presence of undisturbed living organisms exerts a calming effect because the sight of undisturbed animals and plants has been a useful sign of safety during most, if not all, of man's evolutionary history. We know that nonhuman primates use the flight behavior of other animals with more acute senses to signal danger—the sudden agitation of grazing antelope upon catching the scent of a leopard would be a good example of such a warning signal. Thus any animal that has recognizable flight behavior, and flees in the presence of animals that are of danger to primates, can be a signal of safety if it remains tranquil. Moreover, our language and shared symbols continue to use representations of nature undisturbed as signs of safety. For example, undisturbed plant life can be a signal of safety, since plants or trees blown about by storm winds are also a classic visual signal of danger. In contrast, we use the flight of animals as a visual means of indicating the presence of danger in film and television. An especially well-known symbolic representation of the safety of undisturbed animal life is the popular painting "The Peaceable Kingdom" by Edward Hicks, which, inspired by the biblical phrase "And the Lion shall lay down with the Lamb," shows predators and prey at rest with one another. It is therefore not at all surprising that the sight of an aquatic representation of the peaceable kingdom in the microcosm of an aquarium, with its calmly swimming fish and gently swaying plants, can induce relaxation.

## Physiological Responses to the Presence of a Dog

When subjects contemplate an aquarium, the living forms are viewed apart from other human beings. Other experiments tested the effect of pairing a pet dog with a human experimenter; the dog served only as a visual object, and the subjects did not interact with the animal. In one experiment, children were brought into a comfortable living room in which there was a female experimenter, either alone or with a dog. Physiological measurements were taken while the child was silent and while he was reading aloud. The presence of the dog significantly decreased blood pressure, but not heart rate, whether the subject was quiet or reading aloud (Friedman et al. 1983). Interestingly, it has also been found that having the experimenter's dog present in the room reduces the anxiety of subjects as measured by psychological test scales (Sebkova 1978), and that people are more approachable for conversation when accompanied by their dogs (Messent 1983) (Figure 3). Thus, pairing an animal with a strange person can make that person and the entire situation less threatening.

## The Principle of Antithesis

The dog is an interesting companion, in part because it displays clear, unequivocal, and sharply contrasting signals for submissive approach and threatened aggression. Darwin (1872) used the shift in behavior of a dog, from territorial defense at the approach of an apparent stranger to affectionate submission when the person was recognized to be his master, as an illustration of the principle of antithesis.

I would like to offer the hypothesis that natural phenomena which people recognize as intrinsically calming are always one aspect of an opposed pair of visual representations, one signaling danger and the other safety. The greater the contrast, the more valuable the signal. Thus calm and affectionate cats and dogs are contrasted with the same animals in postures of attack. Consider the contrast between the picture of the cat purring by the fire and the tensed shape of the Halloween cat. The sight of waterfowl swimming slowly in a pond is a universal symbol of tranquility, but the rapid and simultaneous flight of a flock of birds from a tree is a warning. Grazing herbivores are idyllic pastoral images, but stampeding cattle signal conflict. This principle of antithesis also extends to inanimate events that can be paired into signals of safety and danger: The fire in the hearth (fire contained) signals safety, while a burning building or

*Figure 3. The presence of a pet dog has been found to contribute to a more relaxed, less threatening atmosphere in human interactions. People have been found to be more approachable for conversation when accompanied by their dogs. (Illustration by Sally Bensusen.)*

forest fire (fire uncontained) signals danger; a gentle surf viewed from the shore contrasts with a raging sea viewed from a vessel.

This principle of antithesis should permit us to develop tests about the selective ability of calm-living animals to attract our attention and calm us. It should not be difficult to electronically generate intricate patterns of motion, having no obvious resemblance to natural patterns of movement, that signal either safety or danger to humans. However, if our hypothesis is correct, these patterns of movement should have significantly less ability to induce feelings of safety and relaxation than natural events.

The unequivocal nature of the dog's signals also suggests why pairing a dog with a human companion should make that person more approachable and less threatening. People are capable of very equivocal and deliberately inaccurate emotional displays, and too many people follow Lady Macbeth's injunction to "Look like the flower but be the serpent under it." The unequivocal signals of many animals provide an unambiguous communication for both the human being and the animal.

### The Calming Effect of Physical Contact

The analysis of visual signals of safety does not imply that only visual contact with animals serves to induce calm. Actual physical contact also plays an important role.

The data from my research show that many people lie down together or sleep with pets. In many cases the people are not sleeping but just resting, apparently enjoying the contact and the serenity of the situation. It should be kept in mind that there are many levels of peaceful consciousness. A good image of this is a person before the fire with a cat resting in the lap or a dog by the side of the chair. One can fill in the image by visualizing the person's hand idly stroking the fur of the animal. That kind of almost unconscious touching is frequently seen when observing how people pet animals (Katcher 1981, Katcher et al. 1983c) and can be described as "idle play." Here the pet becomes an extension of the self. In this kind of interaction, the person's gaze is not fixed on the animal, for at times the eyes may be unfocused as if the person is in reverie, or the eyes may be directed at some portion of the environment but with a low level of attentiveness as might happen when one stares at a fire or an aquarium. The pet's fur is played with, stroked, or rolled between the fingers. These gestures are quite similar to the displacement gestures which children and adults direct toward their own persons during times of tension.

Living things when contemplated or touched not only interrupt our patterns of thought, they also enable us to think with divided attention, so that the character of our thought changes. Reverie is a kind of self-generating thought that comes to us when our attention is divided between the sight of lifelike motion and the workings of our own mind. Bachelard (1956:14) described the reverie that occurs when a person contemplates a fire in a fireplace:

The dream proceeds on its way in linear fashion, forgetting its path as it hastens along. The reverie works with a star pattern. It returns to its center to shoot out new streams. . . . In this case it is a question of the quiet, regular, controlled fire that is seen when the great log emits tiny flames as it burns. It is a phenomenon both monotonous and brilliant, a really total phenomenon: it speaks and soars and it sings. The fire confined to the fireplace was no doubt for man the first object of reverie, the symbol of repose, the invitation to repose.

This creative kind of thought-play may very well also derive from our association with the living world about us, and especially from our observation of and interaction with animals. This point is illustrated by Konrad Lorenz (1952:17–18) in another description of the creative force of reverie:

A man can sit for hours before an aquarium and stare into it as into the flames of an open fire or the rushing waters of a torrent. All conscious thought is happily lost in this state of apparent vacancy, and yet, in these hours of idleness, one learns essential truths about the macrocosm and the microcosm.

# Intimacy

## Pets as "People and Family Members"

Let us now turn to an examination of the ways in which people interact with, and respond to, their own companion animals. The pets of urban Americans are spoken to as if they were people; they are confided in and enlisted as participants in social ceremonies. Many subjects referred to their pets as "members of the family," either spontaneously when explaining why they tolerated undesirable behavior by the pet (Voith 1981), or when they were asked directly in questionnaires (Katcher et al. 1983c, Katcher 1981, Ganster and Voith 1983). My colleagues and I found that those people who designate animals as members of the family have a greater tendency to sleep with, talk to, and confide in the animal, display a photograph or painting of their pet, and celebrate its birthday. They are also more likely to have special clothes, toys, and furniture for the animal. Thus, people behave toward pet animals with some of the social acts that are usually reserved for fellow humans with whom they have a close and friendly relationship.

To explore the nature of this close relationship, we looked at people touching and talking to animals. We observed that the gestures used to touch animals are ones which would be signs of intimacy if directed toward other human beings. Interestingly, we found that men use gestures of intimacy with animals with the same frequency as women (Katcher et al. 1983c, Brown in press), whereas studies of touching between adults in the United States indicate that in public situations women almost always use more intimate touches than men (Goffman 1976).

When we examine how people incorporate cats and dogs in family photographs, we see that they are presented in postures of close physical contact, usually with the head of a person and the animal in contact or close proximity. We examined a geographically stratified sample of one thousand two hundred photographs selected from twenty-five thousand that were submitted to a national photographic contest in which contestants were asked to photograph their pet cat or dog in a family context. Over 92 percent of the photographs showed a diadic relationship: one person and one animal occupying the center of the photograph. Ninety-seven percent of the photographs illustrated people and animals touching each other, and in most instances the head of the animal and human being were close together. Almost *none* of the photographs illustrated the two common ways animals appeared in portraiture before this century: with the animal at its master's feet, or posed with children in a formal family portrait. The human subjects were almost always smiling, and the photographs usually represented the person and animal in the same kind of intimate dialogue we observed in the laboratory. The pictorial representations also reinforced our conclusion from the behavioral data that the animal and person were posing as parent and child (Ruby 1983, Ruby and Katcher 1983, Katcher and Beck 1985).

The dog has been bred to conform to its social role as a kind of child by selective breeding for juvenile characteristics of both facial form and behavior. Humans nurture a variety of living things. This can be looked upon as a kind of play, much like the doll play of children, which was probably originally practiced in preparation for nurturing their own children in adulthood. Later, however, that nurturant play was preserved into adult life and took on new and important functions. For example, human play with the young of wild animals could have been an initial step toward domestication (Savishinsky 1983). We have carried over into our adult life a kind of nurturant behavior that has found a whole variety of outlets, not the least of which is our nurturance of pet animals. At the present time, when fewer people are electing to have children, and when those who do have fewer children, it is not surprising that pets are playing a progressively more important role within the family.

## Human Physiological Changes during Interactions with Pets

My colleagues and I have measured blood pressure and observed overt behavior when people talked to other people and when they talked to their pets. While talking to people invariably produced rises in blood pressure, talking to and touching pets resulted either in no increase or a decrease in systolic blood pressure (Katcher 1981). This observation has subsequently been confirmed by other investigators (Baun et al. 1984). Since that time we have extended our research to include prisoners interacting with birds, cats, and small mammals, with similar results. When these prisoners were talking to and touching their aniamls, their blood pressure was lower than when they were talking to the investigators (Katcher et al. 1983b).

The decreased physiological arousal that accompanies interaction with pet animals, as indicated by a reduction in blood pressure, is also associated with a stereotypical set of changes in facial expression and voice pattern. The face becomes more relaxed, with a generalized decrease in muscle tension especially evident around the eyes and the brow. The smile, which is usually present during interaction, becomes more relaxed with less tension at the corners of the mouth. When speaking to the animal, the person's lips are frequently open and slightly pursed. The voice becomes much softer and higher in pitch, and the speech pattern is broken into a small series of words, often phrased as a question and concluded with a rising intonation. These questions are followed by silent periods in which the person solicits eye contact and answering gestures from the animal. We believe these characteristic patterns of facial expression and voice that accompany interaction with pets may be linked to accompanying measurable changes in blood pressure. There is independent evidence that rapidity of speech is connected with the magnitude of the blood-pressure elevation during speaking (Friedmann et al. 1982). The slower the speech, the less elevation in blood pressure. In fact, patients with labile hypertension have been treated by teaching them to speak more softly and slowly and with more pauses for breathing (Lynch, pers. comm.). Furthermore, Eckman, Levenson, and Friesen (1983) have observed that cardiovascular changes (heart rate and skin temperature) can be produced by muscle movements of the face. When subjects imitated the muscle movements expressive of emotion, the cardiovascular changes were appropriate to that emotion. Hence, the facial muscular changes we observed in people interacting with their pets may be directly linked to the observed cardiovascular changes.

# Conclusion

Contemporary Americans feel that the family of man includes animals, and that animals are treated as the children in that family. Photographs of people and their pets portray intimacy and emotional proximity rather than hierarchical distance. The person and the animal are blended as an expression of the purity and insularity of their relationship. In other discussions of the feelings generated by keeping pets, I have emphasized that caring for pets can generate a sense of constancy even when the rest of human existence seems to be in continual flux (Katcher 1983, Beck and Katcher 1983). Pets provide that sense of constancy because we nurture them without any expectation that they will change, without any demand for progress or perfection. This *contentment with things as they are* distinguishes our attitude toward pets from our demands upon our children, from whom we expect physical, intellectual, and moral growth.

# Select Bibliography

Bachelard, G. 1956. *The psychoanalysis of fire,* trans. A.C.M. Ross. Boston: Beacon Press.

Baun, M.M., L. Thoma, N. Langston, and N. Bergstrom. 1984. The physiological effect of petting and the influences of attachment. In *The pet connection: Its influence on our health and quality of life,* ed. B. Hart, A. Hart, and A. Anderson. St. Paul: Grove Publishing.

Beck, A., and A. Katcher. 1983. *Between pets and people.* New York: G.P. Putnam.

Benson, H. 1980. *The relaxation response.* New York: William Morrow and Co.

Brown, D.S. In press. Some consequences and determinants of human–companion animal relationships. In *Proceedings of the 1983 conferences on the human–animal bond,* ed. B. Hart and R.S. Anderson. St. Paul: Globe Publishing Co.

Darwin, C. 1872. *The expression of the emotions in man and animals.* Reprinted 1965. Chicago: University of Chicago Press.

Eckman, P., R.W. Levenson, and W.V. Friesen. 1983. Autonomic nervous system activity distinguishes among emotions. *Science,* 221:1208–10.

Friedmann, E., A.H. Katcher, S. Thomas, J. Lynch, and P. Messent. 1983. Social interaction and blood pressure: Influence of animal companions. *Journal of Nervous and Mental Diseases,* 171:8, 461–65.

————, S. Thomas, D. Kulick-Ciuffo, J. Lynch, and M. Suginohara. 1982. The effects of normal and rapid speech on blood pressure. *Psychosomatic Medicine,* 44:545–53.

Ganster, D. and V. Voith. 1983. Attitudes of cat owners toward their cats. *Feline Practice,* 13:21–29.

Goffman, E. 1976. Gender advertisements. *Studies in the anthropology of visual communication,* 3:65–154.

Katcher, A.H. 1981. Interactions between people and their pets: Form and function. In *Interrelations between people and pets,* ed. B. Fogle. Springfield: Charles C. Thomas.

————. 1983. Man and the living environment: An excursion into cyclical time. In *New perspectives on our lives with companion animals*, ed. A. Katcher and A. Beck. Philadelphia: University of Pennsylvania Press.

————, A. Beck, E. Friedmann, and J. Lynch. 1983a. Looking, talking and blood pressure: The physiological consequences of interaction with the living environment. In *New perspectives on our lives with companion animals*, ed. A. Katcher and A. Beck. Philadelphia: University of Pennsylvania Press.

————, A. Beck, and D. Levine. 1983b. Prisoners and pets: Evaluation of the Lorton Prison pet placement program. Paper presented to the November 1983 Delta Society Meeting, Washington, D.C.

————, E. Friedmann, M. Goodman, and L. Goodman. 1983c. Men, women and dogs. *California Veterinarian* 37:2, 14–17.

————, A. Beck, and H. Segal. 1984a. Contemplation of an aquarium for the reduction of anxiety. *American Journal of Clinical Hypnosis*, 27:82–85.

————, H. Segal, and A. Beck. 1984b. Comparison of contemplation and hypnosis for the reduction of anxiety and discomfort during dental surgery. *Amer. J. Clinical Hypnosis*, 27:14–21.

————, and A. Beck. 1985. Safety and intimacy: Physiological and behavioral responses to interaction with companion animals, pp. 122–28. In The human–pet relationship: Proceedings of the international symposium on the occasion of the 80th birthday of Prof. Konrad Lorenz, Vienna, Austria.

Lacey, J.I., J. Kagen, B.C. Lacey, and H.A. Moss. 1963. Situational determinants and behavioral correlates of autonomic response patterns. In *Expressions of the emotions in man*, ed. P.J. Knapp. New York: International University Press.

Lorenz, K. 1952. *King Solomon's ring*. London: Methuen.

Lynch, J. Personal communication.

Messent, P.R. 1983. Social facilitation of contact with other people by pet dogs. In *New perspectives on our lives with companion animals*, ed. A. Katcher and A. Beck. Philadelphia: University of Pennsylvania Press.

Ruby, J. 1983. Images of the family: The symbolic implications of animal photography. In *New perspectives on our lives with companion animals*, ed. A. Katcher and A. Beck. Philadelphia: University of Pennsylvania Press.

Ruby, J., and A.H. Katcher. 1983. Ideal and real: Photographs of pets in the family. Paper presented at the November 1983 Delta Society Meeting, Washington, D.C.

Savishinsky, J. 1983. The domestication of animals: Human behavior and human emotions. In *New perspectives on our lives with companion animals*, ed. A. Katcher and A. Beck. Philadelphia: University of Pennsylvania Press.

Shepard, P. 1978. *Thinking animals*. New York: Viking Press.

Sebkova, J. 1978. Senior thesis. Department of Psychology, University of Lancaster, Lancaster, U.K.

Voith, V. 1981. Attachment between people and their pets: Behavior problems of pets that arise from the relationship between pets and people. In *Interrelations between people and pets*, ed. B. Fogle. Springfield: Charles C. Thomas.

# Animals, Evolution, and Ethics

## Gordon M. Burghardt and Harold A. Herzog, Jr.

The lives of humans and animals have always been intimately connected. Animals have been prey, predators, parasites, and competitors of humans. Dozens of species have transported us, worked in our fields, and carried our burdens. They have been our friends, guarded our lives and possessions, and entertained us. But animals have been more than just useful and amusing. They have been incorporated deeply into our emotional and intellectual existence, and have served as religious deities, models of conduct, and symbols in art, literature, and myth. Clearly, turning an objective scientific eye upon our relationship with animals is bound to be difficult and even controversial. But it is important for us, as well as for animals, that we at least attempt to do so.

Over many thousands of years, humans have developed methods of dealing with animals based on observation, induction, and deduction. Our successful hunting and domestication of so many species demanded a basic understanding of their behavior—that "ready-to-hand" (practical) knowledge discussed by Russow (this volume). However, the objective science of animal behavior is a much more recent development stimulated by the serious acceptance of Darwin's theory of evolution by natural selection. People began looking at animals in a new light, because to recognize essential, rather than superficial, similarities between human and nonhuman could no longer be attacked as either unscientific or sentimental.

Several of the chapters in this book provide different perspectives on how animals currently are perceived in our culture. Animals can be considered favorably or negatively: They may be revered or eaten, maligned or studied. While none of these oppositions is necessarily mutually exclusive, all of them pose difficult ethical problems.

The popular term *animal ethics* is ambiguous, since it can refer either to human ethical stances toward animals or to ethical factors that might influence the behavior of animals toward each other. The latter is a far from trivial point, for at the heart of many controversies concerning the obligations and duties humans owe animals is the question of whether animals conduct their own affairs with each other in ways similar to or different from the ways humans deal with each other. Thus an ethical interpretation of the behavior of animals can be used to point to the biological roots of our own behavior as well as to shape our ethical stance toward other species.

These two aspects of animal ethics have become intertwined and often confused over the years. We will not review all of the often insightful writings on evolutionary ethics and on the ethical treatment of animals that began to flower in the late nineteenth century, but we would like to cite a few outstanding examples. More than ninety years ago, E. P. Evans published a book entitled *Evolutional Ethics and Animal Psychology,* which has not been equaled for scholarship and insight. The following quotation is from its first paragraph:

There are scarcely any topics which excite such general interest, and are
so frequently discussed nowadays, as the origin and evolution of ethical
conceptions as revealed in . . . the growth . . . development . . . outward
manifestations and essential qualities of mind in lower animals, . . . the
study of which the most recent researchers in comparative philology, biology, psychology, and kindred branches of natural and mental science have
given a fresh impulse and new direction, and opened up a broader and
clearer field of view. (Evans 1898:2)

Nine years later, Ernest Thompson Seton, one of America's leading
wildlife experts, wrote *The Natural History of the Ten Commandments*
(1907). He evaluated the evidence for the operation of each commandment
in animals and came up with intriguing examples indeed. He was, of
course, using the ten commandments as examples of universal moral precepts with counterparts in all or most human societies. More recently,
Wolfgang Wickler, successor to Konrad Lorenz at the Max Planck Institute
in Seewiessen, West Germany, published a provocative little book entitled
*The Biological Basis of the Ten Commandments* (1974). His goal, method,
and conclusions were remarkably similar to Seton's, although his examples
and their interpretation were often quite different. Obviously people know a
lot more today about animals and how to use and evaluate evidence, but on
the whole we have progressed little in terms of formulating basic questions,
speculating upon answers, and drawing ethical conclusions.

Our goals in this chapter are to outline the problems with developing
a consistent ethical system for mankind's treatment of animals, to speculate upon why resolution of the dilemmas posed by animals is so difficult,
and to begin developing a framework to allow analysis and resolution of
our current ethical dilemmas.

# Ethical Dilemmas

How can we define these? Several years ago, we (Burghardt and Herzog
1980) argued that there were so many competing values currently at work

*Table 1.*

## Considerations Entering into Ethical Evaluation of Relations with Other Species.

| A. Human Benefit | B. Anthropomorphism | C. Ecology | D. Psychology |
|---|---|---|---|
| 1. food | 1. pain and suffering | 1. rarity | 1. habituation |
| 2. clothing | 2. goriness | 2. diversity | 2. aesthetics |
| 3. transportation | 3. phylogenetic similarity | 3. ecological balance | 3. spiritual and religious |
| 4. recreation | 4. humanoid appearance | | 4. call of the wild |
| 5. research | 5. mental similarity | | 5. individual variability |
| 6. pests and competitors | 6. cuteness | | 6. behavioral plasticity |
| 7. danger and disease | 7. size | | |
| 8. domestication | 8. longevity | | |
| | 9. disgusting habits | | |

from Burghardt and Herzog 1980

in our dealings with animals that no consistent ethical system could be devised or even envisioned. The extensive literature on the topic since then (there is now a journal called *Ethics and Animals*) has not altered this conclusion.

Presented in Table 1 is a list of some of the considerations involved in any ethical decision concerning the use or treatment of an animal. Now, it might seem perfectly understandable why people should be antagonistic toward organisms that eat our crops or transmit deadly diseases, or why we should value animals that are companions or, like horses, render so much service and recreational pleasure, but things are not that simple. Cruelty to pet dogs and horses, painful slaughtering methods of cattle and pigs, maintaining highly social primates in barren isolation in research labs, and killing porpoises in the process of catching tuna for our casseroles all illustrate that useful or highly valued species are not always treated with respect and sensitivity.

Many of our inconsistencies are overt and blatant. Few people protest killing ("controlling") rodents that eat crops, but when birds or bunnies are involved the champions of morality turn out in force. When feral animals become destructive to the environment and need to be culled to maintain an ecological balance, some species elicit human outrage while others are ignored.

Threatened burros in the Grand Canyon elicited expensive and dangerous helicopter rescues. At the National Zoological Park's own endangered-animal research center in Virginia, animal protection organizations, but not hunters or ecologists, were in aggressive (and successful) opposition to hunting overpopulated deer that were causing ecological damage and posing a health threat to zoo animals (white tail deer can transmit a fatal brain worm to rare, exotic ungulates). In Great Smoky Mountains National Park, rangers have been killing wild boar for years without a peep from the animal-welfare movement, but with plenty of flak from hunting groups. The hunters finally accepted a grudging compromise that, when practical, killed boar would be used to provide meat to the poor people of the Appalachians, and trapped boar would be released to adjoining National Forests where hunters themselves could kill them. In East Tennessee, environmentalists, ecologists, ichthyologists, and fishermen were most concerned about the snail darter, which was threatened with extinction by the Tellico dam. But there was little expression of support from humane societies, nor did most national environmental organizations haul out their artillery and go beyond ritual support—apparently embarrassed about expending political capital on such a humble little fish.

We do not recount these examples to claim that one side or the other is right or wrong, nor do we advocate consistency for its own sake. It would be naive to propose that animal-welfare organizations should broaden their scope to include every species, or that conservation organizations should not discriminate among the species and habitats they try to save. Nor is the answer vegetarianism, stopping all animal research, outlawing wild pets, or buying only organically grown foods—all of which have been seriously advanced by major theoreticians. These examples merely show that neither the conservation nor the animal-protection movement has an ethical stance comprehensive enough for all the difficult choices that confront us. This is also true of farmers, veterinarians, scientists, and government wildlife services, which have scarcely begun serious ethical discussions of principles for animal treatment (although veterinary medicine schools are becoming more aware of some of the dilemmas facing their profession: For example, are veterinarians beholden to their patients, the animals, or to their clients, the humans who pay the bills?).

# Factors Influencing Ethical Decisions

Not everyone will respond the same way to all the considerations listed in Table 1 when they are confronted with an ethical question concerning animals. Indeed, that is part of our point. What, then, are some of the factors that influence the ethical stances people take toward animals? Factual information is certainly important (although later we will question its singular role). Educating people about biology may be essential in reducing conflicts over the ethical treatment of animals.

For years the creation/evolution debate has fascinated us. When one of us (GB) first moved to Tennessee, the antievolution law was still on the books and the Scopes trial had taken place nearby. In 1982 GB decided to poll his students on their attitudes toward animals and evolution, with a very brief twelve-item survey (Figure 1) to foster discussion. The results so intrigued GB that he has since surveyed other classes as well as scientists, veterinarians, church groups, and others. Here we will discuss only those results dealing with the relationship between attitudes.

From the data obtained on item 5 (Figure 1), we compared those who agreed, or agreed with reservations, that evolution is a fact, with those who disagreed or strongly disagreed, and found that the two groups also responded significantly differently to *every other item* (see Tables 2a and 2b). Thus a simple survey like this shows that one's acceptance of evolu-

# Animals, Evolution, and Ethics

STUDENT SURVEY

Please fill out this form and leave in the boxes as you exit

The questions are meant to be a quick way of determining general attitudes.
I well realize that many of you might prefer to see different wording or
a more extensive attempt to delve into these complex issues.  However, do
the best that you can quickly.  It will be greatly appreciated.

Answer by checking the box that most closely represents your views.

*strongly agree — agree with reservations — disagree — strongly disagree*

1. Many nonhuman animals are similar to us in their feelings and emotions. ☐ ☐ ☐ ☐

2. Many nonhuman animals are similar to us in their intellectual capacities. ☐ ☐ ☐ ☐

3. Many nonhuman animals are similar to us in their normal behavior patterns. ☐ ☐ ☐ ☐

4. Nonhuman animals are too greatly different from us to make any comparisons useful. ☐ ☐ ☐ ☐

5. The occurrence of evolution is a fact (i.e. as certain as most generalizations in science ever are). ☐ ☐ ☐ ☐

6. The occurrence of evolution is only a theory that is still questionable on scientific grounds. ☐ ☐ ☐ ☐

7. The most widely accepted mechanisms of evolution (natural selection, mutation, etc.) are only theoretical speculations. ☐ ☐ ☐ ☐

8. Science tells us nothing about the 'purpose' of our lives or values and morality. ☐ ☐ ☐ ☐

9. We are insignificant blobs in a chaotic universe. ☐ ☐ ☐ ☐

10. In its details the creation account in The Bible is incompatible with modern science. ☐ ☐ ☐ ☐

11. (a)  I have a personal conflict in reconciling my religious beliefs on divine creation with evolutionary biology. ☐ ☐ ☐ ☐

    (b)  Even thinking about the issue bothers me. ☐ ☐ ☐ ☐

12. Do you consider yourself primarily a Biologist ☐ or Psychologist? ☐

THANK YOU FOR YOUR
COOPERATION

Gordon M. Burghardt
Dept. of Psychology
University of Tennessee
Knoxville, TN   37996

*Figure 1. A twelve-question survey designed to determine the general attitudes of college students toward animals and evolution.*

135

*Table 2a.*

## Analysis of Survey Responses (%) to the First Four Statements in Figure 1.

1. Many nonhuman animals are similar to us in their feelings and emotions.

|  | SA | AR | D | SD | N |
|---|---|---|---|---|---|
| *Accept Evolution* | 25.4 | 53.0 | 18.9 | 4.7 | 455 |
| *Deny Evolution* | 14.7 | 46.3 | 22.0 | 17.0 | 177 |

$$x^2 = 19.17, p < .0003$$

2. Many nonhuman animals are similar to us in their intellectual capacities.

|  | SA | AR | D | SD | N |
|---|---|---|---|---|---|
| *Accept Evolution* | 12.0 | 37.8 | 34.7 | 15.5 | 458 |
| *Deny Evolution* | 3.8 | 26.4 | 42.9 | 26.9 | 182 |

$$x^2 = 25.25, p < .0001$$

3. Many nonhuman animals are similar to us in their normal behavior patterns.

|  | SA | AR | D | SD | N |
|---|---|---|---|---|---|
| *Accept Evolution* | 27.9 | 55.6 | 12.9 | 3.6 | 451 |
| *Deny Evolution* | 14.2 | 48.6 | 25.1 | 12.0 | 183 |

$$x^2 = 38.99, p < .0001$$

4. Nonhuman animals are too greatly different from us to make any comparisons useful.

|  | SA | AR | D | SD | N |
|---|---|---|---|---|---|
| *Accept Evolution* | 3.8 | 7.8 | 41.0 | 48.2 | 461 |
| *Deny Evolution* | 12.8 | 22.4 | 27.5 | 17.3 | 179 |

$$x^2 = 76.70, p < .0001$$

(derived from Burghardt 1985)
The critical factor is whether the respondents accept or deny evolution as a fact (statement 5, Figure 1). SA = strongly agree; AR = agree with reservations; D = disagree; SD = strongly disagree.

*Table 2b.*

## Analysis of Survey Responses (%) to the Eighth Statement in Figure 1.

Science tells us nothing about the "purpose" of our lives or values and morality.

|                  | SA    | AR    | D     | SD    | N   |
|------------------|-------|-------|-------|-------|-----|
| *Accept Evolution* | 28.1  | 27.2  | 30.5  | 14.2  | 459 |
| *Deny Evolution*   | 48.9  | 22.3  | 19.0  | 9.8   | 184 |

$$x^2 = 26.26, p < .0001$$

(derived from Burghardt 1985)

The critical factor is whether the respondents accept or deny evolution as a fact (statement 5, Figure 1).

tion has a pervasive effect upon attitudes that will affect ethical decisions. And accepting evolution also has an effect upon one's views as to where values come from (Table 2b). This indicates that there will be reluctance to allow scientific input to modify what are perceived to be values by large segments of our population.

How, then, do we arrive at a sound ethical system for dealing with animals? Certainly not by simply intuiting a system that may satisfy us as individuals. Not only is it impossible for a person to be consistent, but the value judgments we make are affected by deep-seated, often emotional, but also rather subtle values, such as a belief in the conservation ethic, which might influence our behavior and attitudes in hidden ways.

This is also true of our treatment of other people. One of the basic questions raised by ethical philosophers is whether ethical precepts reflect universal principles that exist outside our self- or group interest. The recent tendency has been to see religious precepts not as divinely inspired but as products of human reason or guises for pursuing self-interest. Thus it is easy to show the reason why not eating pork or holding cows sacred arose in certain cultural settings. And ethicists, going back to Socrates, have posed disturbing questions about rigid adherence to moral precepts.

For example, Socrates asked (Singer 1981), Is it always right to return what you have borrowed? Socrates' companion replies, Of course. But suppose, asks Socrates, it was a weapon that was borrowed, and the owner is now deranged and may endanger others if he gets it back?

The point is that every one of the ten commandments may under some circumstances be abrogated with rather clear consciences by devout Christians and Jews—even the most serious one, "Thou shalt not kill." People use this latter precept to oppose war, abortion, and the death penalty, but virtually no one will not admit the need for violent behavior against other humans under some conditions. And almost no one seriously applies this to all animals. Even Albert Schweitzer killed snakes near his hospital, and the more irreverent have claimed he did away with excess kittens as well! There are no simon-pure saints.

If morality does not lie outside of ourselves in either supernatural dogmas or universal cosmic principles, where *does* it lie? Are ethical precepts just individual preferences codified to grease our slide through life? Are our approaches to animals nothing but culturally determined habits and symbol manipulation? Let us, for argument's sake, use some evolutionary thinking here: not meaning the influence that knowledge and acceptance of evolution might have on our values, but rather the possibility of going beyond the apparent irrationality of many common attitudes to postulate some plausible biological mechanism or survival value which could have caused "ethically related" responses to evolve through natural selection.

The other chapters in this volume amply demonstrate the many idiosyncratic ways in which humans relate to animals in this and other cultures. This diversity seems to suggest varying cultural influences on our treatment of animals—for instance, bears and snakes may be feared, eaten, or revered. Yet let us entertain the notion that below the surface of such variation lies a deeper genetically shaped reservoir of tendencies, preferences, predilections, and emotions that are shared by all humans and perhaps by other species as well, insofar as the forces of natural selection have acted similarly upon them. It is also possible that many of our responses to animals derive from our hunter–gatherer heritage. Such responses may be as much genetic as cultural.

E. O. Wilson (1978) and other sociobiologists as well as numerous earlier evolutionists have claimed that values, just like perceptual systems and behavior, may be under the influence, if not the control, of our evolutionary heritage. If this is so, then many of our ethically related views concerning animals might eventually be understood (though not necessarily condoned) by looking at evolutionary forces. Furthermore, evolutionary ethical considerations might turn out to be an essential part of the eventual resolution of ethical dilemmas concerning animals.

Let us take the list of considerations in Table 1 and categorize them in a different way, by their value orientation (Table 3). Some of the items—for example, the use of animals in research or for transportation—bring in rational issues whose connection with any evolutionary forces is indirect at best. The ethical issues, however, revolve around considerations such as pain, size, and cuteness, which do have some connection with natural selection. The evidence is of two types: 1) evidence of innate, unlearned responses, or the ability to quickly learn things; and 2) plausible scenarios suggesting that the value-related consideration could have been produced or influenced by natural selection. The latter type of evidence is less satisfactory than the first. Overlying all of these factors is the issue of familiarity and habituation—sensitization due to prior exposure—which we will not directly address, but which are ubiquitous psychological processes found in virtually all animals.

Now we would like to discuss some animals and topics about which people have strong feelings—feelings that to a greater or lesser extent may have been influenced by natural selection. We will offer some hypotheses as to why such feelings arise.

# Animals and Topics that Elicit Strong Feelings in Humans

### Fear of Snakes

Whether the fear of snakes is learned or innate has been asked for many years (Figure 2). As snake enthusiasts ourselves, we used to think that the environmental argument had it: People were afraid of snakes because of the

*Table 3.*

## Proposed Value Attributions of the Major Considerations Influencing Animal Treatment.

| Consideration | General Value Attribution | |
|---|---|---|
| | *Positive* | *Negative* |
| 1. adult appearance | humanoid | alien |
| 2. juvenile appearance | cute (baby releasers) | lack of baby releasers |
| 3. juvenile behavior | awkward, playful | precocious |
| 4. phylogenetic relationship | close | distant |
| 5. size | large | small |
| 6. intelligence | smart | dumb (also sly or cunning) |
| 7. habits | nice | nasty |
| 8. communication method | reliance upon vision and audition within our range | reliance upon odors, touch, vision or audition outside our abilities |
| 9. reaction to injury | struggling, cries, whimpers, "red blood" | immobility, no audible vocalizations, different innards |
| 10. method of killing | neatly dispatched | gory, slow |
| 11. life span | long-lived | short-lived |
| 12. reproductive rate | low | high |
| 13. population size | rare | common |
| 14. geographic distribution | restricted | ubiquitous |
| 15. aesthetics | pretty, graceful | ugly |
| 16. individual variability | much | little |
| 17. level of zoomorphism | bonding to individuals, "friendly" behavior | responds same way to all people; fearful, passive, or ignores people |
| 18. perceived danger to humans | little or none | venomous, "vicious," disease-transmitting |

| 19. competition for resources | little overlap | exploits livestock, crops, game, fisheries |
| 20. domestic animals | being used for purposes congruent with domestication history | use for purposes other than those behind domestication |
| 21. direct exploitation (e.g., food, clothing, transportation, research, recreation) | use OK if seen as valuable or necessary | use attacked if seen as trivial or dispensable |

*Figure 2. Copperhead. The fear of snakes exhibited by humans has been debated for years. Once viewed as a learned response, there is now some evidence that the fear may be innate.*

biblical story of the serpent and the apple. It now appears that the human fear of snakes may be an unlearned phenomenon (Morris and Morris 1965) that also occurs in other primates when learning has been excluded. Why should humans and other primates be afraid of snakes? The answer may be that snakes readily access trees—man's old habitat—and certain species are poisonous and deadly; large constrictors can also pose dangers to

141

human young. Before guidebooks were available, being slow to identify a snake might have proved unfortunate—indeed, one could have been selected out in an evolutionary sense, especially in Asia and Africa where there are no simple rules for quickly identifying poisonous snakes as there are in the United States. Thus we see no problem in ascribing the fear of snakes, and also spiders, of which a few are deadly, to genetic factors. The consequences of curiosity could kill more than a cat.

## Humanoid Features

The attractiveness of some animals can best be explained by the similarity of their form and facial features to ours. But this is a relatively modern attitude. Even in the nineteenth century, chimps, orangutans, gorillas, and monkeys were viewed as ugly, vicious, degraded animals whose likeness to people of European descent made a mockery of God's care in creating humans. For most Europeans and Americans, true public appreciation of primates awaited the growth of tolerance and acceptance of nonwhite races as legitimate members of the "human race." However, positive valuation of humanoid features in certain animals may not be extended to alien peoples, even other ethnic groups (subraces) within one race, due to equally biologically based fears.

## Baby Releasers

The appeal of juvenile animals has long been recognized, although it was Konrad Lorenz (1950, see 1971) who analyzed the specific features of human infants found in the young of other animals that are the basis of the response. Our response to "cute" animals is surely based on the generalization of parental-care responses that were essential to the survival of mammals in general and humans in particular.

## Juvenile Behavior

Some aspects of juvenile mammal behavior are as appealing as cute looks. One of us (GB) remembers being enchanted by the awkward movements of a newborn moose at the Milwaukee Zoo. Now, the moose is not your standard cute animal, not even when young, but its behavior was irresistible. So is animal play. Animals that play seem to be valued more than those that do not, especially if we can readily interpret the behavior as play. Again, our attraction to these attributes could be based on genetic predispositions to attend and respond to juvenile humans. Awkward young children need our safeguarding and attention, while those that are precocious and adultlike, apparently needing us less, may be ignored.

## Phylogenetic Closeness

This factor is again based more upon the anthropomorphic or humanoid features of our close relatives than upon their actual evolutionary relationship. Humans might react more favorably to bear cubs than to infants of the alien-appearing, big-eyed tarsier, a strange little nocturnal primate from Southeast Asia.

## Size

Human preference, all else being equal, is for large animals (Figure 3). Part of the reason for this seems to be our own relatively large size as well as our perceptual limitations, but other more practical factors may be involved. Tiny animals such as flies tend to be very common, and small animals are less likely to be useful—too small to eat, train, play with, make clothes out of, and so forth. Large animals are more likely to live longer, be less fecund, have smaller population sizes, be smarter, and have more individuality— all aspects that would favor them for food and domestication. We know many scientists who work with insects; we know none who has developed any emotional bonds with his subjects, as is common among those who work with mammals, birds, and even reptiles and fish.

## Longevity and Reproductive Rate

We think it was in early man's interest to favor long-lived, slowly reproducing animals. Overexploitation of them would have more disastrous effects.

143

*Figure 3. African elephants. Humans seem to show a preference for large animals. This may be a result of the fact that humans are relatively large compared to other animals. (Illustration by Richard Swartz.)*

The implication is not that early humans, or any humans, are or were good ecologists, but that some advantages would accrue to individuals or tribes that were more conserving of their resources. The fact that so many people could so rapidly become environmentally conscious and emotionally committed in recent years may argue for there being an innate if buried basis for this response. With certain key inputs, the response, a stabilizing, conservative one, is triggered.

## Rarity and Population Distribution

Rare animals typically are favored. This may seem somewhat arbitrary, since the pain of a common species, say a cow, is no less than the suffering of a poached wild ungulate, but we do treat the two differently. Again, while knowing that various species are endangered is intellectually transmitted knowledge, our concern for them, often so emotional, may be derived from the value placed on rare animals in our early history. The last of anything is always more valued. Such animals or their parts played important roles in rituals, costumes, medicine, and elevated social status.

Our easily instilled concern for animals found only in restricted habitats may have evolved from the needs and experiences of hunter–gatherer societies and may have a biological component. However, some species may be very plentiful in a small restricted area, say an island, and often vulnerable to overexploitation.

## Intelligence

People value *smart* animals, if we have not first discredited their brains by labeling them sly, deceitful, or cunning. As with our evaluation of other people, certain kinds of intelligence are favored in animals. Animals that can perform tasks humans recognize as complicated are valued. (See for example the descriptions of the piano-playing pig, card-playing macaw, and basketball-playing raccoon in Breland-Bailey 1986.)

## Habits

We like our animals to behave with proper decorum. Basically this is anthropomorphic projection of our values onto the animal. A selling point for wolves is that they are loyal to the pack, and such good parents, too— the father even helps out, and we know how rare that is in mammals! Porpoises are especially admired because they rescue one another, and are even credited with saving drowning humans. One may well ask whether this selective anthropomorphism by the promotors of particular animals is appropriate, or whether it is cheap and exploitative. In the long run, such attitudes might damage the chances of animals for which we cannot find effective anthropomorphic "tags".

## Communication Method

People are much more sensitive to the whimpering cries of puppies than to the high-frequency screeches of baby bats. And we have no sensitivity at all to the pheromones given off by frightened rats. In our evolutionary history we evolved sensory abilities to deal with *our* problems, not those of other animals. Thus we are inescapably biased toward species with which we can at least have the illusion of empathizing or communicating.

## Pain and Suffering

Humans are most sympathetic toward the suffering of animals that respond as we think we might in similar circumstances. Those to which we cannot relate we ignore, such as when we boil lobsters, spray irritative poisons on cockroaches, hook fish, and so on. Furthermore, our response to the methods of killing animals is biased, so that gory, slow deaths are particularly abhorrent. Vegetarians, however, often point out that every animal we eat is deprived of its life even if killed painlessly. The more astute animal-rights philosophers know that the pain issue will not evoke much sympathy because each of us rationalizes the issue in his or her own way.

## Competition

Animals that have been competitors for resources in the past, such as wolves and raptors, bear the brunt of bad feelings. People who have had direct experience with a competing species, and have suffered real or imagined losses, quickly develop great antipathy for the species. While this can be irrational and not adaptive, one can see how it came about. First, mobilizing one's hate could have been necessary to save one's crops, herds, even family. Such emotions, once established, are hard to eradicate.

## Domestication

Are specific genetic forces behind our response to domesticated species? There might have been selection for individuals in families who most effectively tamed or cared for domestic stock. Research has shown that farm animals given individual attention and perceptive care are more productive and healthier than those given more mechanical, impersonalized care. Could not the extraordinary care and devotion people lavish on farm animals and pets be derived, not just from seeing them as child substitutes and members of the family, but also from natural selection for *human* characteristics related to successful animal husbandry? What we need are studies of villages in underdeveloped countries to see if those people who are more attentive to their animals are more successful in reproducing them.

## Variability

Animals that vary in behavior and morphology seem favored. They have "personality." Might this be an evolved preference? Domestication of animals itself necessitates close and careful observation of traits in animals. Perhaps our interest in variability is derived from a comparable need to be observant of people.

## Zoomorphism

Animals that bond with us as individuals are favored—animals that act as if they think we are both of the same species. Dogs are the best example, with their strong bonding tendency developed from their wolf-pack ancestry. Cats might seem to be an exception, but they often do like to be petted and sometimes sleep with their owners. Cats and dogs both adapt well to humans, discriminate friend from foe, and have many endearing behavior patterns directed toward people: Dogs wag their tails, cats purr, and so on. Fowl and sheep might seem more impersonal until one recognizes the emotional impact the tagging along of an imprinted chicken, duck, or lamb has on a human. Through filial behavior they can compensate for other less endearing traits.

Pets can in some ways be considered toys. Play is often viewed as the rehearsal of adult behavior (Fagen 1981), and children may learn or practice skills in raising pets that put them at a selective advantage as farmers, hunters, or parents.

147

Aesthetics

The sense of beauty may seem difficult to understand biologically, but aesthetics and morality are closely linked. True, our tastes in art and nature may vary so wildly that to claim some innate character seems ludicrous— for example, some people find snakes and iguanas beautiful while most people shrink away. But throughout history people seem to have been attracted to many of the same animal forms: butterflies, colorful birds, majestic mammals. Perhaps further research in the area of aesthetics will identify the particular attributes that attract people, since it appears to be specific features, rather than specific organisms, that we find attractive.

# Biological Basis for Human Attitudes toward Animals

This quick survey of factors that can influence our attitudes toward animals should serve to show that many of our apparently value-laden attitudes toward animals may be based on innate biological predispositions. These may derive from our genetically evolved responses to fellow humans, or from the survival value that certain attitudes toward animals had for humans. Either of these, insofar as it corresponds to reality, has profound implications for the possibility of altering our behavior. Many thinkers (e.g., Singer 1981) claim that it is reason that makes us ethical. Perhaps, however, reason has merely given us the ability to understand our own basic patterns of behavior and to make minor adjustments. If an ethical system does not have a survival value for its adherents, it will wither away. Consider religions whose practices led to environmental degradation, reduced survival, or nonreproduction. The Shakers are no more, despite some very attractive doctrines, because they banned producing children. In Tennessee there are still fundamentalist churches where the faithful handle venomous snakes and drink poisons. We may respect, even admire, their faith, but few of us will follow suit and thus the practices will die out along with the faithful. Thus an ethical system for animals will only be successfully implemented by any human group to the extent that it does not deter human survival.

Evolutionary ethicists should be careful not to argue from *what is* to *what ought to be,* but it is equally fallacious to argue that either condition could exist independent of our biological nature and needs. Moreover, our evolved attitudes towards animals contain the motivational, emotional, and intellectual resources necessary to devise a successful program for the ethical treatment of animals.

# Conclusion

Moral controversies seem to erupt only over those uses of animals that are not universally accepted in society. Eradicating mice, cockroaches, and termites from our houses is never a source of controversy because no one really wants them there. Now, some people may prefer to trap mice and rats alive, but most debates revolve around the safety of poisons to humans and pets, not the moral rights of ants, termites, rats, or mice. We need to look at those treatments of animals that are *not* controversial to uncover common ground for resolving ethical dilemmas. When we talk to groups and ask them to give an example of a moral dilemma they commonly face concerning animals, we almost always get an example such as putting down a pet or slaughtering a favorite farm animal. Lesser but still significant levels of concern are expressed for chimps and whales, but essentially none is offered for undescribed species of insects being exterminated as rain forests disappear. Ethical prescriptions, then, apply to preferred individual animals. Concern for species or habitats with which we have developed some bond are a distant second. Abstract appeals to save all of nature are not only vague but will never work.

Singer's (1981) general guidelines for ethical rules are as applicable to our dealings with animals as they are to our interactions with each other. Such rules need to be personal, involve education of the young, have limited obligations, reduce the need for intricate calculations of costs and benefits, control the tendency to bend ethical calculations in our favor, and foster truthfulness. Furthermore, ethical rules should derive from shared means, values, and ends, but should also respect a person's short-term but very real concerns involving his livelihood. We must appeal to the good in humans, to their basic sensitivity to animals—encourage and foster it, and confront with public debate questionable uses of animals. But we must avoid the polarizing righteous indignation that does not respect the human values and concerns of those with different views. Our concern should be the animals, not just catharsis for our own guilt or outrage.

We must also realize that no simple answer, no one system will suffice. We might combine the best aspects of Kellert's various typologies (this volume) by paring them down to three categories: *anthropomorphic empathy, conservation ethic,* and *utilitarian consequences.* Each conflict that arises could then be evaluated from each of these perspectives and the critical basic assumptions exposed. Unresolvable conflicts may simply reflect rigid thinking. Our educational strategies must include training to break the tendency to evaluate an issue from only one perspective.

A change in attitudes and behavior can occur in several ways, although rarely does change occur solely as a result of new factual information. It may come about accidentally, by continual bad consequences that literally force change; but the most important vehicle of change is lateral thinking, which involves breaking out of our rigid thought patterns to see new ways of addressing a problem. We have tried to apply lateral thinking in this chapter by exploring the assumption that our ethical values may be genetically influenced, to see where that idea leads. Perhaps such an approach will help us to see some of our current ethical dilemmas in a new light.

# Select Bibliography

Breland-Bailey, M. 1986. Every animal is the smartest: Intelligence and the ecological niche. In *Animal intelligence: Insights into the animal mind*, ed. R. J. Hoage and L. Goldman, 105–14. Washington, D.C.: The Smithsonian Institution Press.

Burghardt, G.M. 1985. Animal awareness: Current perceptions and historical perspective. *American Psychologist* 40:905–19.

————, and H.A. Herzog, Jr. 1980. Beyond conspecifics: Is Brer Rabbit our brother? *BioScience* 30:763–68.

Evans, E.P. 1898. *Evolutional ethics and animal psychology.* New York: Appleton.

Fagen, R. 1981. *Animal play behavior.* New York: Oxford University Press.

Lorenz, K. 1971. *Studies in animal and human behavior, Vol. II.* Cambridge, Mass.: Harvard University Press.

Morris, R., and D. Morris. 1965. *Men and snakes.* New York: McGraw-Hill.

Seton, E.T. 1907. *The natural history of the ten commandments.* New York: Scribners.

Singer, P. 1981. *The expanding circle: Ethics and sociobiology.* New York: Farrar, Straus and Giroux.

Wickler, W. 1974. *The biology of the ten commandments.* New York: McGraw-Hill.

Wilson, E.O. 1978. *On human nature.* Cambridge, Mass.: Harvard University Press.